E. L. Dooley

1970

Disciple Preaching in the First Generation

An Ecological Study

Cordially,

Dwight E. Stevenson

Disciple Preaching
in the
First Generation

An Ecological Study

by

Dwight E. Stevenson

The Forrest F. Reed Lectures
for 1969

THE DISCIPLES OF CHRIST HISTORICAL SOCIETY

NASHVILLE, TENNESSEE

1969

MANUFACTURED IN THE UNITED STATES OF AMERICA

Preface

The purpose of the Forrest F. Reed Lectures is to tell it like it was, so we may help to keep it like it ought to be. Our Committee this year chose as the speaker Dr. Dwight E. Stevenson and asked him to speak on some phase of the history of preaching among the Disciples of Christ. His original and creative proposal to deal with preaching in this approach met with unanimous approval.

Among all the heirs of the Campbell-Stone movement, preaching is the growing edge of our Christian experience. We understand better our origins as well as our present drives when the sermons revealing the mind-set of our pastors are analyzed as Dr. Stevenson has done in these lectures.

Since "preaching is the communication of truth through personality," these lectures share with us the mature scholar-

68702

ship of an irenic spirit, laying possibly a foundation for the future when we shall again become "one flock with one shepherd." God speed the day when all who love Christ shall prove the reality of that love by the way they treat each other!

ROBERT W. BURNS, *Chairman*

Wayne H. Bell
Willis R. Jones
Roscoe M. Pierson
Forrest F. Reed
Hugh M. Riley

Foreword

The Forrest F. Reed Lectureship was established October 3, 1964, and is held annually under the auspices of the Disciples of Christ Historical Society. Funds for its endowment were given through a permanent trust created by Forrest F. Reed, Disciples layman of Nashville, Tennessee, and a member of the Board of Trustees of the Historical Society.

By action of the Board, the Lectureship has been named in honor of its donor. Its purpose, as described in the trust agreement set up by Mr. Reed, is to provide "a series of lectures by history scholars objectively interpreting some phase of (Disciples) church history."

Forrest F. Reed was Chairman of the Nashville Planning Committee which brought the Disciples of Christ Historical Society to Nashville in 1952. He has been a member of the Board of Trustees since 1952, and was Chairman from July 1, 1962, through June 30, 1966.

Dwight E. Stevenson has been associated with Lexington Theological Seminary, Lexington, Kentucky, since 1947, as

7

Professor of Homiletics and now as Dean of the Faculty. Both as teacher and as author he has gained a national reputation. As author or as collaborator he has some twenty books to his credit.

Dr. Stevenson is a graduate of Bethany College where he served as head of the Departments of Religion and Philosophy from 1944 to 1947. He received his B.D. degree from Yale and did special graduate study at the University of Chicago. In 1947 Bethany College conferred upon him the honorary D.D. degree.

Selected to deliver the fourth series in the annual Forrest F. Reed Lectures, Dr. Stevenson brought both disciplined scholarship and great personal charm to his assignment.

WILLIS R. JONES, President-Curator
DISCIPLES OF CHRIST HISTORICAL SOCIETY

Contents

I

From Lands Across the Sea

Ecology in science is that branch of biology dealing with the relation between organisms and their environment. When applied to preaching, ecology is the relation between sermons and their "context" or "situation." The term was first used in this sense by Joseph Sittler as title for his Yale Lectures, *The Ecology of Faith.*[1] We have heard a great deal lately about "Situational Ethics" and "Contextual Ethics," which simply means that you do not pursue the question of right and wrong in a sociological vacuum. The same may be said for preaching. The world-setting of a contemporary sermon, Disciple or otherwise, is altogether different from that on the American scene between the Revolutionary and the Civil Wars. Disciple preaching of that early period cannot be understood apart from its social and cultural background. We can say even more than that: Disciple sermons of the 1830's are different in kind from those of the 1960's, not simply because of what they are in themselves, but also—and more especially—because of the relation they bear to their cultural environment.

---

[1](Philadelphia: Muhlenberg Press, 1961).

11

To the extent that sermonic literature is available from the early period, there is a temptation to deal with the printed sermons of the fathers as self-sufficient entities and to judge them by supposedly timeless homiletical standards. If we fall into such a temptation, we commit not one but two errors. On the one hand, we make the sermons of the fathers irrelevant to their own times. Whatever they were, they were not that! And, on the other hand, since there is no such thing as an undated homiletical theory equally valid for all epochs of history, we unwittingly try to force the preaching of the fathers into the mold of our twentieth-century models. Thus, for example, we can easily indict the fathers because they did so little pastoral preaching and because they relied so heavily on argumentation and debate. Or, to give still another example, we innocently place all their sermons in the setting of the formal worship service at eleven o'clock on Sunday morning in an imposing ecclesiastical edifice. In the beginning, such a setting was so exceptional as to be almost nonexistent!

Unless we distort history-writing and reading into a crippling misadventure, we have simply got to make the attempt to divest ourselves of our twentieth-century world, our presuppositions, our concerns and battle lines. We had better warn ourselves at the outset that we are going to be only partially successful in such disrobing; we will cling to at least some shreds of modern clothing with which to cover our nakedness. But we must try. More than that, we must also try to robe ourselves with the presuppositions and concerns of the fathers, and move into their world and out onto their battle lines and frontiers.

This is even harder to do. The vital issues of yesterday, which involved everybody in battle, involve us as little more than interested or sleepy spectators yawning over the late show. Meantime, we have our own battle lines, our own growing edges, our own tortured notion of "where the action really is" in this our own time. And we marvel that our fathers could have been so wrought up over issues that interest us so little.

The truth is that the battle of life rages without truce or armistice from one generation to another and that it is fundamentally pretty much the same battle—against ancient wrongs and for the acquisition of new lands. But the fronts of this eternal warfare keep shifting from one sector to another. This happens not once but many times in a generation or a lifetime, as anyone over fifty years of age surely knows. Life has to be defined in terms of engagement—at its frontiers, or growing edges—where the present, sensitive, tender, and vulnerable, is eating its way into the unknown and untried future. Therefore, the background question which you must ask and never cease to remember about any historical period, our own included, is this: Where is the battlefront? Upon what frontier are men now marching off their old maps? Unless we can ask that question and answer it to some degree by walking into the picture and becoming contemporary with them *in their concerns and struggles,* we will never know what they were doing.

Early Disciple preaching, as delimited for these lectures, will be taken to mean preaching up to the time of the Civil War. This was the formative period. As such it is basic. It has entered into our heritage, and, as the boy enters into and merges with the man he becomes, it has entered into us. For this is another observation that we must make about yesterday's frontiers: They become today's heartlands.

When one considers Disciple preaching in relation to its environment in that period, he finds it opening up to him under three headings: (1) derived from the Old

World, (2) addressed to the New World, (3) in the light of a new vision.

DERIVED FROM THE OLD WORLD

There is really nothing in our contemporary experience that quite matches the migration of our fathers to the American continent. With the spread of the automobile, having acquired wheels in place of legs, we have become nomads wandering from place to place, looking for the most inviting grasslands. But our fathers were not nomads. The rise of new tyrannies has recently driven hundreds of thousands of refugees to our shores from Germany and Hungary and Russia. But our fathers were not displaced persons, driven from one settled country to another. Times past have seen the mass movements of peoples invading, conquering, and appropriating high civilizations—as the Hyksos kings did in subduing Egypt, and as the Goths and Visigoths did in occupying the house that Rome had built. But our fathers were not mere invaders.

To understand our fathers when they were still in Europe, it would be necessary for us to wake up tomorrow morning to a world in which the work of exploration and discovery was still unfinished. A world into which there erupts one common day the news of a whole new continent, rising whole and inviting out of the waters of the western sea. No crowded world already overrun, tamed, and despoiled by predatory man, its prairies are unbroken by the plow, its forests untouched by ax or saw, its rivers and streams unbridged and unpolluted, its vast expanse unmapped, uncrossed by road or rail, its rich veins of ore untapped. It is a virgin land, fresh as Eden on the morning after creation. Drop that into your awareness, and suddenly you are drawn as by an earth-sized magnet. You become a pilgrim and a pioneer. For that is what our fathers were—pilgrims and pioneers. To reflect their sense of history, they went back to biblical roots and interpreted their migration to America through the symbols of the Promised Land and the conquest of Canaan:

> O God, beneath Thy guiding hand
> Our exiled fathers crossed the sea;
> And, when they trod the wintry strand,
> With prayer and psalm they worshipped Thee.
> Laws, freedom, truth, and faith in God
> Came with those exiles o'er the waves;
> And where their pilgrim feet have trod,
> The God they trusted guards their graves.[2]

The discovery of such a virgin world would be equaled today only by the return of space-voyaging astronauts telling us that Mars is not only inhabitable but also unimaginably inviting—plus the news that Cape Kennedy will shortly establish regular passenger service at prices within the reach of the family budget.

For our migration to Mars, in spite of its inviting prospects, we will need more than a million pounds of thrust to blast us loose from our earth moorings and overcome the gravitational pull of old loves and loyalties. Moreover, when we set out for the new, we cannot succeed in leaving everything old behind. We will go in the clothing of earthlings, speaking an earthling's language, carrying an earthling's Bible, with a whole conceptual world inside our heads designed, manufactured, and copyrighted on earth. And when we begin settling Mars and building up its civilization—in spite of all our efforts to the contrary—we will begin duplicating what we had on earth. So Mars will be populated in time by its New Nashvilles, its New

---

[2]Leonard Bacon, "The Pilgrim Fathers."

Clevelands, and its New New Orleans and its New New York! Mars with its different kind of gravity and its own unique atmosphere and climate calls for something very different, but, like the Dutch, building winter houses in the tropics of the East Indies, we will cling to what we knew and give only grudging place to a culture indigenous to the climate.

Something like this is what happened to our fathers. They left the old world behind them. They blasted themselves loose from it decisively, irrevocably. They set out, drawn only by the promise of the new. But they carried the old with them, on their backs, in the holds of their ships, but most of all in their minds. In nothing was this more true than in the character of their religious faith and practices.

THE PROTESTANT REFORMERS

They came to these shores, first of all, as Protestants. Alexander Campbell clearly recognized this and joyously acknowledged it. In the Preface to *The Christian System* he wrote:

> We Americans owe our national privileges and our civil liberties to the Protestant Reformers. They achieved not only an imperishable fame for themselves, but a rich legacy for their posterity. When we contrast the present state of these United States with Spanish America, and the condition of the English nation with that of Spain, Portugal, and Italy, we begin to appreciate how much we are indebted to the intelligence, faith, and courage of Martin Luther and his heroic associates in that glorious reformation.[3]

Under a topic, "The Remission of Sins," well into the same volume Campbell again paid his respects to this

---

[3]A. Campbell, *The Christian System, in Reference to the Union of Christians, and a Restoration of Primitive Christianity, as Plead in the Current Reformation* (St. Louis: John Burns, n.d.), p. 3.

Protestant heritage. In fact, he opened the chapter with the following paragraph:

Luther said that the doctrine of justification, or forgiveness, was the test of a standing or falling church. If right in this, she could not be very far wrong in any thing else; but if wrong here, it was not easy to suppose her right in any thing. I quote from memory, but this was the idea of that great reformer. [Here he added a footnote for a later edition quoting Luther from a commentary on the Epistle to the Galatians: "The reformer also said: 'If the article of justification be once lost, then is all true Christian doctrine lost.'"] We agree with him in this as well as in many other sentiments. Emerging from the smoke of the great city of mystical Babylon, he saw as clearly and as far into these matters as any person could in such a hazy atmosphere. Many of his views only require to be carried to their legitimate issue, and we should have the ancient gospel as the result.[4]

Decades later Isaac Errett spelled out Disciple agreements with the Protestant doctrine in some detail.

There is scarcely anything recognized by [Protestants] as essential or vital, that is not as truly and firmly held by us as by them. We are one with them in holding to and advocating the following items of doctrine:
1. The divine inspiration of the Holy Scriptures of the Old and New Testaments.
2. The revelation of God, especially in the New Testament, of the tri-personality of Father, Son and Holy Spirit.
3. The alone-sufficiency and all-sufficiency of the Bible, as a revelation of the divine character and will, and of the gospel of grace by which we are saved; and as a rule of faith and practice.
4. The divine excellency and worthiness of Jesus as the Son of God; his perfect humanity as the Son of man; and his official authority and glory as the Christ—the Anointed Prophet, Priest and King, who is to instruct

[4]*Ibid.*, p. 179.

us in the way of life, redeem us from sin and death,
and reign in and over us as the rightful Sovereign of
our being and Disposer of our destiny.[5]

Having sketched these broad agreements with all Protestants, Errett then got down to particulars by naming
thirteen points of doctrine in which Disciples saw eye-to-
eye with all sects and denominations within Protestantism: The Incarnation, Christ as final revelation, the
Atonement, Resurrection, Ascension, the Lordship of
Christ, Holy Spirit, the "alienation of the race from God,
and their entire dependence on the truth, mercy and
grace of God . . . for regeneration . . ." the necessity of
faith and repentance, Baptism and the Lord's Supper as
perpetual ordinances, the Lord's Day, the Church as divine, Christian morality, the universality of the gospel,
and the final judgment.[6]

Such a catalog was offered as an impressive demonstration of solidarity with Protestantism. Several points of
agreement "with some but not all" Protestants offered
later in the same pamphlet further deepened this solidarity. All of these agreements appeared in the content of
Disciple preaching.

Beyond that, however, the Protestant heritage showed
up in the importance assigned to preaching in the Disciple movement. Luther and Calvin with their weighty
emphasis upon the indispensable role of the oral word of
the preacher did not accord it a higher honor than the
reformers of the nineteenth century. Campbell and his
associates were preachers tirelessly engaging in their
craft.

One index to the importance they assigned to preach-

---

[5]Isaac Errett, *Our Position: A Brief Statement of the Plea for a Return to
the Gospel and the Church of Apostolic Times, Urged by the People Known
as Disciples of Christ* (Cincinnati: Standard Publishing Co., n.d.), p. 3.
    [6]*Ibid.*, pp. 3-4.

ing is the frequency with which they preached. It was considerably more than a single sermon, on a single day of the week! The Protestant reformers preached so often as to astonish us. As John H. Nichols expresses it, "All of them preached prodigiously. In most of the Reformed communities [that is in Calvin's movement] there were two or three sermons on the Lord's Day and several during the week, sometimes daily. The appetite for the Word preached was startling by modern standards, both in length and solidity of sermons and the number of them desired by the congregations. For the twelve thousand people of Geneva there were fifteen services with sermons every week. . . ."[7]

The same sort of thing happened among the Lutherans. A report on preaching at Wittenberg shows not one but three sermons on Sunday: one on the epistle for the day at five or six o'clock in the morning, a second on the gospel for the day at eight or nine o'clock, and a third in the afternoon when the preacher took up the books of the Old Testament one after the other and went through them in consecutive sermons week after week. Throughout the rest of the week there were sermons every day: Mondays and Tuesdays, the sermons were based on catechism, or decalogue, or creed, or the Lord's Prayer, or the sacraments; Wednesdays they were from Matthew; Thursdays and Fridays they were from the Epistles; Saturdays they were from the Gospel of John. Not all of this was done by one man, for Wittenberg had a staff of preachers—Luther and three or four assistants.[8]

---

[7]John Hastings Nichols, *Corporate Worship in the Reformed Tradition* (Philadelphia: Westminster Press, 1968), p. 29. Used by permission of Westminster Press.

[8]H. Richard Niebuhr and Daniel D. Williams (eds.), *The Ministry in Historical Perspectives* (New York: Harper & Row, 1956), pp. 131-132 in "The Ministry in the Time of the Continental Reformation" by Wilhelm Pauck.

Dargan informs us that Luther himself sometimes preached as many as four times a day, that in 1529, to cite one year, he preached regularly three or four times a week. In 1541 he preached four times on Sunday, two or three times during the week, and twice on holy days. His two hundred sermons on the Book of Deuteronomy were delivered in little more than a year.[9]

Regarding Zwingli, Howard G. Hageman informs us:

The schedule of services in Zwingli's Zürich is not without interest. Every Sunday as well as every festival day (Zwingli retained the celebration of all the major festivals) there were morning services at seven and an afternoon service at three in each of the four parishes. In addition, at eleven on Sundays there was a children's service in the Cathedral only. Daily services were held in each church at 5:00 A.M. and 8:00 P.M. Every morning at eight Zwingli conducted in the Cathedral the "Prophesying," a meeting in which a Biblical passage was discussed not only by the preacher but by members of the congregation as well. Those who think two services on Sunday and a midweek meeting an intolerable burden should consider that in Zürich a minister preached fourteen times in a week. Fortunately Zwingli thought that no service should last more than an hour.[10]

John Wesley proved himself a genuine heir to these continental reformers by his own practice. Early in 1739 he wrote in his Journal:

Every morning I read prayers and preached at New-gate. Every evening I explained a portion of Scripture at one or more of the societies. On Monday, in the afternoon I preached abroad near Bristol; on Tuesday, at Bath and Two-Mile-Hill alternately; on Wednesday at Baptist Mills; every other Thursday near Pensford; every other Friday in another part of Kingswood, on Saturday in the

---

[9]Edwin C. Dargan, A History of Preaching (Grand Rapids: Baker House, 1954), p. 370.

[10]Howard G. Hageman, Pulpit and Table (Richmond: John Knox Press, 1962), p. 22. Used by permission of John Knox Press.

afternoon and Sunday morning in Bowling Green (which lies in the middle of the city): on Sunday, at eleven, near Hannam Mount; at two, at Clifton, and at five on the Rose Green.[11]

We are given to understand that he followed a schedule like that for fifty years. Of course, as he got older, he had to slow down a little! When he was eighty-five (in 1789), he wrote in his Journal: "My sight is so decayed that I cannot well read by candle-light; but I can write as well as ever; and my strength is much lessened, so that I cannot easily preach above twice a day."[12]

That was the heritage that our fathers brought with them from Europe and Great Britain. They lived up to it. This we see from a few samplings of the record of Disciple preaching on the frontier: Walter Scott wrote from Versailles, Kentucky, in 1847: "I have preached and spoken three times a day for a week."[13] J. T. Johnson, U. S. congressman turned evangelist, wrote his daughter September 6, 1854, "In ten weeks I have spoken upward of 100 times."[14] "Raccoon" John Smith wrote "Father" Stone in the early 1830's, "I preach almost every day, and immerse at every meeting; and sometimes I preach and immerse twice a day."[15] William Hayden, in thirty-five years as an evangelistic preacher, was reported to have traveled ninety thousand miles on horseback and to have preached more than nine thousand sermons, "which is two hundred and sixty-one discourses per annum for

---

[11]*Wesley's Journal*, ed. N. Curnock (New York: Philosophical Library, 1951), p. 72.

[12]*Ibid.*, p. 415.

[13]William Baxter, *Life of Elder Walter Scott* (Cincinnati: Bosworth, Chase and Hall, 1874), p. 335.

[14]John Rogers, *Biography of Elder J. T. Johnson* (Cincinnati: By Author, 1861), p. 339.

[15]*Christian Messenger*, VII, p. 251.

every year of his public life. He once preached fifty sermons in the month of November alone."[16]

A MEDIEVAL TOUCH

The influence of Europe and the British Isles showed
up in still another way in the preaching of the Disciple
fathers. That was in the matter of sermon structure. Curi-
ously enough, the heritage here was out of the Middle
Ages, which managed somehow to leapfrog the imposing
figure of Martin Luther and reestablish itself at the front
of the column in the seventeenth and eighteenth cen-
turies. Classical sermon form, as we may call it, was a
product of Aristotelian logic applied by the preaching
orders—an outgrowth of Roman Catholic scholasticism.
Even the early American Puritans, who supposedly rejected both their Episcopal and their Roman heritage,
were influenced by it: A Puritan preacher first "opened"
the text in its context. Next, he "divided" the text, drawing profitable points of doctrine from the divisions as he
unfolded them. Finally, he "applied" the text to the lives
of the people; this last step was sometimes called the
"uses" of the text.[17] This Puritan form was nothing more
than a simplified transmission of that classical form. We
see it, for example, in the outline given by Charles
Simeon, an early contemporary of John Wesley: Simeon
insisted that a proper sermon should have five parts—
"the exordium or introduction, the connection or context,
the division of the text, the discussion by textual divisions,
and the application."[18] The "application" or "uses" of the

---

[16]Baxter, *ibid.*, p. 209.

[17]Winthrop S. Hudson, "The Ministry in the Puritan Age." in *The Ministry in Historical Perspective* by H. R. Niebuhr and D. D. Williams (New
York: Harper, 1956), p. 189.

[18]Jean Claude, "An Essay on the Composition of a Sermon," in *Landmarks in the History of Preaching* by Bishop Yngve Brilioth (London:
S.P.C.K., 1950), p. 36. Used by permission of S.P.C.K.

text followed a fairly definite pattern, based upon the joining of 2 Timothy 3:16 with Romans 15:4: "All Scripture is given by inspiration of God, and is profitable for doctrine, for reproof, for correction, for instruction in righteousness." "For whatsoever things were written aforetime were written for our learning, that we through patience and comfort of the Scriptures might have hope." Thus the fivefold "uses" which were employed in whole or in part in every sermon embraced "information, reproof or confutation, education, correction, and consolation."[19]

While there was much in the Disciple movement to cause them to push off from this heritage, the fathers were more influenced by classical homiletical form than we would have expected. Take the most famous Disciple sermon of them all as example—"The Sermon on the Law" delivered by Alexander Campbell September 1, 1816.[20] This sermon has a text, Romans 8:3, "For what the law could not do, in that it was weak through the flesh, God, sending his own son in the likeness of sinful flesh, and for sin, condemned sin in the flesh." In a brief exordium (or introduction) Campbell dealt with the importance of understanding the term "law" in its biblical context. He then "divided" the text:

"In order to elucidate and enforce the doctrine contained in the verse, we shall scrupulously observe the following

METHOD

"1. We shall endeavor to ascertain what ideas we are to attach to the phrase *'the law,'* in this, and similar portions of the sacred scriptures.

"2. Point out those things which *the law* could not accomplish.

---

[19]*Ibid.*, pp. 22-23.
[20]And as reported by its author in *Millennial Harbinger,* 1846, pp. 493-521.

"3. Demonstrate the reason why *the law* failed to accomplish these objects.

"4. Illustrate how God has remedied these relative defects of *the law*.

"5. In the last place, deduce such conclusions from these premises, as must obviously and necessarily present themselves to every unbiased and reflecting mind."[21]

The first four points constitute the "division of the text," the fifth point presents itself as the "applications" or "uses" of the text—all in true homiletical form. We even discover that the text of this particular sermon has exactly five uses. Here they are: (1) "there is an essential difference between law and gospel. . . . The former waxed old, is abolished, and vanished away—the latter remains, lives, and is everlasting."[22] (2) Christians are not under law, but rather are under gospel. (3) "there is no necessity for preaching the law in order to prepare men for receiving the gospel."[23] (4) All motives and rites drawn from the Mosaic Law "are inconclusive, repugnant to Christianity, and fall ineffectual to the ground. . . ."[24] (5) We are enjoined to receive Jesus "as the Lord our righteousness, and to pay the most punctilious regard to all his precepts and ordinances."[25] When matched against the traditional "uses," the Sermon on the Law will be seen to have supplied all five of them: information, confutation, education, correction and consolation!

We should not be surprised that Alexander Campbell followed classical models in sermon preparation—especially in his early years.[26] After all, he was taught how to

---

[21]*Millennial Harbinger*, p. 496.

[22]*Millennial Harbinger*, p. 508.

[23]*Millennial Harbinger*, p. 508.

[24]*Millennial Harbinger*, p. 520.

[25]*Millennial Harbinger*, p. 520.

[26]See also Robert Richardson, *The Memoirs of Alexander Campbell* (Philadelphia: Lippincott & Co., 1871), Vol. 1, pp. 317-322.

preach by his father, who had been taught in Divinity Hall by Archibald Bruce at Whitburn, Great Britain. Space and time permitting, I could demonstrate a like influence of classical sermon form upon the preaching of all the Disciple fathers, including Barton W. Stone. This is not to say that they always followed it, especially as they moved into a distinctive plea. In some respects they came to react vehemently against the tradition, but they began with their homiletical roots in the soil of Medieval Europe. They were, after all, university men; and the universities which they or their mentors attended were the universities of the Old World.

Robert Richardson in *The Memoirs of Alexander Campbell,* affords us a glimpse into the discipline of sermon form as practiced by Thomas Campbell in teaching his son: "The rules, indeed, were very proper, being founded upon correct principles, both of logic and of rhetoric, which were already familiar to Alexander, and readily reduced to practice. It became, accordingly, almost an invariable custom with the father and the son, after having heard each other's discourses, to examine and test them upon their return home by the established rules."[27]

WESTERN RESERVE—AND ZÜRICH, SWITZERLAND

This workshop approach to the analysis of sermons following their delivery was applied in the Mahoning Baptist Association in the Western Reserve in the 1820's and 1830's, with Campbell's hearty approval and participation. He called it "The School of Preachers." Several ministers held an annual meeting lasting about a week in which each man preached to the general public, then met with his fellow ministers in a closed session in which his ser-

---

[20]And as reported by its author in *Millennial Harbinger,* 1846, pp. 493-

mon was subjected to critical scrutiny and analysis. Regarding the "School" Alexander Campbell wrote in 1835:

> At present there is no means of improvement but in the
> slow and gradual development of the school of experi-
> ence, aided by the censures and criticism of the more
> discriminating of society, and frequently these are not
> the most friendly to their improvement; for these criti-
> cisms, commendations, and censures are not made to
> themselves, so not designed for their benefit; but they
> are either publicly expressed or secretly whispered to
> their disadvantage.[28]

When I first learned about the School of Preachers, I
thought I had found something unique in the early Disciple movement. And then I read more into the history of
the Protestant Reformation, and I learned that the notion
of a preacher's workshop evidently began in Zürich in
1525. It was called "prophesying," the reference being to
Paul's advice in 1 Corinthians 14:29-33, "Let two or three
prophets speak, and let the others weigh what is said. . . ."
(RSV) We are informed that "In Zürich the preachers of
the city gathered in the cathedral five days a week for
their school of prophets. A selected passage was examined
in Latin and Hebrew and Greek. Then its use in a sermon
was discussed and finally a sermon was preached on it."[29]
Similar schools of prophets were held in Geneva and in
London. "In Elizabethan England," we learn, "ministers
gathered in certain counties at a central church and engaged in exposition, one after another, of a selected passage. Questions from the congregation were also enter-
tained."[30] Here is one more instance of the rather
extensive cargo of religious ideas and practices which
our founding fathers carried in their baggage when they
migrated to the New World.

---

[28]*Millennial Harbinger*, 1835, pp. 478-479.
[29]James Hastings Nichols, *op. cit.*, p. 33.
[30]*Ibid.*

THE ENGLISH ENLIGHTENMENT

Much that has entered into the Disciple heritage for preaching was derived from the Old World—much more than we have realized. Much was derived from the Protestant Reformers—Zwingli, Luther, Calvin. Some things were even derived from the Pre-reformation Church. Even then we are not finished with our bill of indebtedness to the Old World. To it we must now add the English Enlightenment. Some years after the cow ate Alexander Campbell's French textbook, thus gaining "more French in her stomach than the boy had in his head," he proved to be considerably less sleepy over the books of John Locke. He was seventeen when he read Locke's *Essay Concerning the Human Understanding*. He also read *The Reasonableness of Christianity* and *Letters on Toleration*. And, since his father was also his teacher, we may be sure that father and son discussed them fully and in some depth. Locke's philosophy furnished the philosophical context of Campbell's theology of preaching in many particulars.

In his *Essay* Locke had set out to demolish the doctrine of innate ideas—the belief that the mind is born with truth in it which may be drawn out by a process of reasoning or "remembering." In place of that old theory of knowledge, he set up another—that the mind is a blank tablet at birth and that all its subsequent ideas come primarily through the five senses. There is nothing in the mind, he insisted, that was not first in the senses. This meant, of course, that the mind is fairly reliable in dealing with facts, but that it cannot be trusted with metaphysical speculations about ultimate questions such as God, Freedom, and Immortality. Immanuel Kant later expressed this same skepticism in a figure. There are some people, he said, who imagine that because a bird can fly through the air it should also be able to fly through interstellar space. The mind simply is not that kind of bird! One obvious inference, and the one that Locke and Campbell made, is that religious truth cannot be reached by human reason; it has to be mediated to us by revelation. Moreover, that revelation must come in a form that the five senses can apprehend—through words and deeds that can be witnessed. Locke, and Campbell after him, went so far in insisting upon the primary value of the senses that they reasoned that Jesus chose fishermen as his disciples because they had good eyes and ears and would become reliable reporters.

Campbell showed his complete sympathy with John Locke's position when he wrote in *The Christian System:*

> Now, be it observed, that, as by our five external senses we acquire all information of the objects of sense around us; so by testimony, divine or human, we receive all our information upon all facts which are not the objects of immediate exercise of our five senses upon the things around us.[31]

One amusing view expressed by Walter Scott in *The Gospel Restored,* and assented to by Campbell, was that before his fall Adam did not need to believe there was a God because he knew and talked with him face to face, whereas after the fall Adam became Lockian man, capable only of sensual knowledge and of faith based on evidence. This led very naturally to Campbell's otherwise astounding statement: "There is not a spiritual idea in the whole human race that is not drawn from the Bible."[32]

In *The Reasonableness of Christianity* Locke had declared that Christianity was a revelation, but that it was not therefore out of accord with reason. It could not have been originated by the human mind, but once it had been disclosed, the human mind could grasp it. In this same

---

[31]*The Christian System*, p. 112.
[32]*Ibid.*, p. 15.

book Locke had also said that creeds, canons, and councils are superfluous as centers of religious authority. The New Testament is the only center of authority and reason its only arbiter. A study of the New Testament, in turn, will disclose that the essential article of faith is the acknowledgment of Christ as Messiah. If a man accepts Christ, he accepts all Christ's teachings. The persuasion which leads toward the acceptance of Christ is based upon evidence of three sorts, all appealing to reason: (1) Christ's miracles, (2) his fulfillment of Old Testament prophecy, and (3) the testimony of Scripture.

In his two *Letters on Toleration,* Locke vehemently repudiated all ecclesiastical authority. One can almost hear Campbell's later essays on the Hierling Clergy as echoes to this Lockian theme. Alexander Campbell called Locke "the great Christian philosopher," and Robert Richardson, his first biographer, wrote that Campbell "read Locke's works early in life, adopted his system of philosophy, and ever afterwards continued to hold it."

Richardson, in fact, felt that Campbell's veneration for Locke was a great handicap to the Disciples. He wrote, in a private letter to Isaac Errett under date of July 16, 1857:

> The philosophy of Locke with which Bro. Campbell's mind was deeply imbued in youth has insidiously mingled itself with almost all the great points of the reformation and has been all the while like an iceberg in the way—chilling the heart and benumbing the hands, and impeding all progress in the right direction.[33]

Whether weight or wings, Locke's philosophy was undoubtedly integral to Campbell's thinking, and especially to his theology of preaching. Since there is not time or space to develop an exposition of that theology here, I am

---

[33]Cloyd Goodnight and Dwight E. Stevenson, *Home to Bethphage* (Bethany Press, 1949), p. 123.

reserving it for a later lecture. It is appropriate to observe, however, that such a theology leaves absolutely no room for direct revelations of the Holy Spirit to the unregenerate heart; consequently, it changes the whole character of evangelistic preaching from that advocated generally in the Great Awakening and the Great Revival. Of that also, more later.

TWO DUTCH THEOLOGIANS

Another philosophical strand which came from the Old World to be woven into the thought of the Campbells was the "Covenant Theology" of the Dutch theologians, Cocceius and Witsius. It was a theology which had deeply penetrated the Seceder Presbyterian Church in Scotland and Ireland. As members of that religious body, the Campbells were, of course, fully exposed to it. As W. E. Garrison shows in his *Theology of Alexander Campbell,* Covenant Theology corrected standard-brand Calvinism at three points: (1) It made a distinction between dispensations in God's dealings with men; (2) it developed a new method of biblical interpretation; and (3) it presented in the covenant idea the assertion that man, as one party to the covenant, had a definite part to play in his own salvation.

Campbell was drawing directly on the first of these positions in his "Sermon on the Law" in 1816 as he made his disturbing distinction between Law and Gospel, and again in 1826 when he preached to the Mahoning Baptist Association on "The Progress of Revealed Light" and developed his subject in four points, referring to four ages: The starlight age of the patriarchs, the moonlight age of Jewish national religion, the twilight age of John the Baptist and the earthly ministry of Jesus, and the sunlight age of the Holy Spirit and the church.

Regarding biblical interpretation, Cocceius wrote sentiments on exegesis which are now very familiar. He said that the plain and obvious meaning of a passage of scripture is to be taken; that words are to be understood in their ordinary sense, without symbolism and allegory; that they must be read in their full context; and that the books of the Bible are to be studied in their historical setting as connected wholes. Campbell's preface to his modern speech translation of the New Testament in 1826 does not surprise us with the statement that the reader "will apply the same rules of interpretation to these compositions which he would apply to other writings of the same antiquity."[34] Chapter II on "The Bible" in his *Christian System* elaborates hermeneutical rules coming directly out of the Covenant tradition.

The covenant aspect of the theology of Cocceius and Witsius was also influential on the Disciple fathers. In fact, the idea that man and God both have their proper roles to play in regeneration is nowhere more completely incorporated into the Disciple pattern than in Walter Scott's plan of salvation. Man does three things: he believes, repents, and is baptized; whereupon God does three things: he remits sin, bestows the Holy Spirit, and gives life eternal. This same theology is also evident in the forthright repudiation of the Calvinistic view of predestination, election, and prevenient grace which enabled a sinner to respond to the Gospel.

THE SCOTTISH INDEPENDENTS

The Scottish Independents had mediated the Covenant Theology to Campbell, but that was not the end of their influence upon the Campbell movement. There is little doubt that Alexander Campbell's approach to church or-

---

[34]Alexander Campbell (ed.), *The Sacred Writings of the Apostles and Evangelists of Jesus Christ, Commonly Styled The New Testament* (Pittsburgh: Forrester and Campbell, 1839), Sixth Edition, p. 12.

ganization and his view of the ministerial office began within the fellowship of the Independents. While he was at the University of Glasgow during the school year of 1808-9, he came under the influence of Greville Ewing, in whose company he spent many long evenings. This influence finally resulted in his severing ties with the Seceder Presbyterians. When he arrived in America in the summer of 1809, he was an Independent.

I shall not attempt to weave the strands of influence into a single fabric, but there were several of these. For example, John Glas about 1727 left his ministry in the Church of Scotland and in time organized a dozen or so independent congregations which emphasized the autonomy of the local church, a weekly communion, the plurality of elders, and lay leadership in worship.[35] The Haldane brothers were active at the time of Campbell's attendance at Glasgow, although Greville Ewing was drifting away from them because he could not follow them into their insistence upon baptism by immersion. Nevertheless, it was the Haldane influence that Ewing mediated to Campbell, with some modifications. It had been the purpose of the Haldanes to restore the exact pattern of the primitive church in structure, ministry, ordinances, and worship. This included foot washing, the holy kiss, and closed communion.[36] Walter Scott, while a member of the Haldane congregation in Pittsburgh for seven years from the spring of 1819 until the summer of 1826, participated in these practices.[37] In fact, he appears to have continued the practice of foot washing as a family rite for visitors to his home in afteryears.

---

[35]W. E. Garrison, *An American Religious Movement* (St. Louis: Bethany Press, 1945), pp. 20-21.

[36]W. E. Garrison and A. T. DeGroot, *The Disciples of Christ: A History* (St. Louis: Bethany Press, 1948), pp. 52-53.

[37]Dwight E. Stevenson, *Walter Scott: Voice of the Golden Oracle* (St. Louis: Bethany Press, 1946), p. 24.

William Ballantine, one of Haldane's evangelists, had written a "Treatise on the Elder's Office" in which he argued for a plurality of elders in every church and insisted upon the practice of mutual exhortation by all the lay members of the congregation as the best means of obtaining elders. This mutual exhortation was regarded not as a mere privilege, but as a duty of all the members. This, as Richardson reported, caused great disorder in the public worship of the Independents and all but destroyed the pastoral office.[38] Ewing seems to have followed Ballantine in a slightly modified way; he introduced, "besides the Lord's Day meeting . . . a weekly church meeting, which was for social worship and mutual exhortation."[39] Ewing had previously adopted the practice of weekly communion.

Thus we see that all or nearly all of the essential elements of Campbell's early stand on church order were supplied by the Independents. Richardson characterized Alexander's stand in 1824 as the adoption of the "weekly breaking of the loaf," the fellowship [the offering], the simple order of public worship, and the independence of each church under the care of bishops or elders. This order was in effect at Wellsburg, Brush Run, and Pittsburgh.[40]

There is a good deal of evidence to support the belief that Campbell was little attracted to the Haldanian emphasis upon mutual exhortation. He favored it, but he felt that it should be safeguarded by placing it under the strict supervision of qualified elders. The following incident, related by Richardson, is instructive:

About this period Mr. Scott was one day accompanying Mr. Campbell on his way from Pittsburgh home, and

---

[38]*Memoirs of A. Campbell*, I, 180.
[39]*Ibid.*, 179.
[40]*Ibid.*, II, 125.

they attended together the meeting of the church at Cross Roads, in which the order of the Pittsburgh Church had been to a considerable extent adopted. A number of the members having read various Scriptures and spoken at length, Mr. Scott was finally called upon to say something. With this invitation he at once complied, by boldly taking the ground that it was unscriptural to have so many teachers, that the liberty conceded was carried to license, and that each member should be confined, according to the Scripture analogy of the human body, to the particular function for which he was best fitted. At the close of his remarks he inquired with emphasis, in the broad Scotch he sometimes used, "What, my brethren! is the Church to be a mouth?"[41]

Richardson tells us that Campbell "fully concurred in the justness of Mr. Scott's admonitions." He then went on to say:

He [Campbell] entirely approved mutual exhortation and instruction, but thought it best that a general permission to speak should be confined to private or social meetings of the church, and that at the Lord's Day meetings, when the public were expected to attend, only those would be set forward who were best able, from their knowledge of the Bible and their natural gifts, to speak acceptably and profitably to the assembly.[42]

This led him to increased emphasis upon the authority of the elders or bishops and to insist that they be paid.

In the present lecture we have only begun to set early Disciple preaching in context. Many of the influences entering into it were derived from the Old World: the basic doctrines of the Protestant Reformers, their emphasis upon the importance of preaching, the frequency with which they engaged in it, and the schools of prophecy in which they sharpened their talents; classical homiletical forms, vaulting over the backs of the Reformers, and

---

[41]*Ibid.*, II, 126-127.
[42]*Ibid.*

bringing Medieval practice to bear in sermon structure; the English Enlightenment; the Covenant Theologians; and the Scottish Independents.

What Disciple preaching was to become could not be predicted from any one of these influences or any combination of them. A new kind of yeast entered the dough. With a voyage across the western ocean in the days before steam and motor ships and the settling of a virgin continent, all of these forces from the Old World were subjected to the transmutations, creations, and confrontations of the New World. In his monumental *Study of History*, Arnold Toynbee wrote a noteworthy section on "The Stimulus of New Ground." The challenge of new land, it seems, is always enormous and is usually transforming, but "such stimulus [is] specially marked in cases where the new ground is separated from the old by a sea voyage."[43]

> These overseas migrations have in common one and the same simple fact: in transmarine migration the social apparatus of the migrants has to be packed on board ship before it can leave the shores of the old country, and then unpacked again at the end of the voyage. All kinds of apparatus—persons and property, techniques and institutions and ideas—are subject to this law. Anything that cannot stand the sea voyage at all has to be left behind, and many things—not only material objects —which the migrants do take with them, have to be taken to pieces, never perhaps to be reassembled in their original form. When unpacked, they are found to have suffered "a sea change into something rich and strange."[44]

---

[43]Arnold Toynbee, *A Study of History.* Abridgment of Volumes I-VI by D. C. Somervell (New York: Oxford University Press, 1947), p. 103. Used by permission of Oxford University Press.
[44]*Ibid.,* p. 104.

II

The Stimulus of New Ground

It is hard for us to move back to the spirit of America at the dawn of the nineteenth century. Threading our way through a multilevel interchange where superhighways are stacked on top of each other like pretzels in a heap, we can scarcely imagine the untracked wilderness. Or standing on the shores of the western sea trying to fill up the Pacific with our tears because there are no more worlds to conquer, we can scarcely get an intimation of the frontier enthusiasm that exhilarated our pioneer forefathers. And yet, unless we can recapture something of their excitement as they set foot on new ground, we cannot even begin to understand them or anything they did, their preaching included.

When the Disciple movement began, America had already passed through the age of exploration and colonization and was passing into the age of expansion. Only one year before the *Last Will and Testament of the Springfield Presbytery*, the Louisiana Purchase had nearly doubled the size of the country, adding land stretching from the Gulf of Mexico to what is now the Canadian border, and from the Mississippi River to the Rocky Mountains. Only one year after the signing of the *Declaration and Address* by Thomas Campbell and the Christian Association of Washington (Pa.), Florida was purchased from Spain. The Oregon Country was added just ten years after the Disciples founded their first college. Texas was acquired in 1845, while Alexander Campbell was in his prime. And the acquisition of New Mexico, Arizona, and California in 1847, two years before our first national convention, completed the dominion of the United States of America "from sea to shining sea." It was not merely that our Disciple fathers set foot on new ground, but that the very land beneath their feet was growing at that time into a great continent and a new nation.

It was not only that the United States was a new nation, but that our fathers saw it as a new kind of nation. As George Washington said in a letter to the Hebrew Congregation of Newport, Rhode Island, on August 17, 1790:

> The Citizens of the United States of America have a right to applaud themselves for having given to mankind examples of an enlarged and liberal policy, a policy worthy of imitation. All possess a like liberty of conscience and immunities of citizenship. It is now no more that toleration is spoken of, as if it was by indulgence of one class of people that another enjoyed the exercise of their inherent natural rights. For happily the government of the United States, which gives to bigotry no sanction, persecution no assistance, requires only that they who live under its protection should demean [deport] themselves as good citizens, in giving it on all occasions their effectual support.[1]

Note how this is reflected in a part of what Thomas Campbell wrote in 1809 in the "Address" section of *The Declaration and Address:*

> The favorable opportunity which Divine Providence has put into your hands, in this happy country, for the accomplishment of so great a good [the reunion of Christians], is in itself, a consideration of no small encourage-

---

[1]In Edwin Scott Gaustad, *A Religious History of America* (New York: Harper & Row, 1966), p. 125. Used by permission of Harper & Row.

ment. A country happily exempted from the baneful influence of a civil establishment of any peculiar form of
christianity—from under the direct influence of the
anti-christian hierarchy—and at the same time, from any
formal connection with the devoted [doomed] nations,
that have given their strength and power unto the beast;
in which, of course, no adequate reformation can be accomplished, until the word of God be fulfilled, and the
vials of his wrath poured out upon them. Happy exemp-
tion, indeed, from being the object of such awful judgments. Still more happy will it be for us, if we duly
esteem and improve these great advantages. . . . Can the
Lord expect, or require, anything less, from a people in
such unhampered circumstances—from a people so liber-
ally furnished with all means and mercies, than a thor-
ough reformation, in all things civil and religious, according to his word? And would not such an improvement
of our precious privileges, be equally conducive to the
glory of God, and our own present and everlasting good?
The auspicious phenomena of the times, furnish collateral
arguments of a very encouraging nature, that our duti-
ful and pious endeavours shall not be in vain in the
Lord.[2]

That Alexander Campbell shared his father's enthusiasm for his new country cannot be doubted by anyone
who reads the letter written December 28, 1815, to his
Uncle Archibald who was still living in Newry, Ireland.
A part of that letter reads:

I cannot speak too highly of the advantages that the
people of this country enjoy in being delivered from a
proud and lordly aristocracy; and here it becomes very
easy to trace the common national evils of all European
countries to their proper source, and chiefly to that first
germ of oppression, of civil and religious tyranny. I have
had my horse shod by a legislator, my horse saddled,

---

[2]W. E. Garrison and A. T. DeGroot, *The Disciples of Christ: A History*
(St. Louis: Bethany Press, 1948), p. 60. Used by permission of Bethany
Press.

my boots cleaned, my stirrup held by a senator. Here is
no nobility but virtue; here there is no ascendance save
that of genius, virtue and knowledge. The farmer here
is lord of the soil, and the most independent man on
earth. . . . No consideration I can conceive of, would induce me to exchange all that I enjoy in this country,
climate, soil and government, for any situation which
your country can afford. I would not exchange the honor
and privilege of being an American citizen for the position of your king.[3]

In "Sermons to Young Preachers—No. IV" published in
The Christian Baptist for April 5, 1830, Alexander Campbell wrote as a man still under the spell of American
opportunity. One can feel the throb of it coursing through
his blood:

The world, many think, is too old, and men have reflected so deeply on all subjects that there is nothing to
be originated, and little advance to be made in any de-
partment of thought. This is a great mistake. The last
four hundred years have done more, by new discoveries
and inventions, to improve human circumstances, than
the twelve hundred years before. There is scarcely any
thing of which it can be said, this is altogether new. New
combinations, and new associations of ideas, and new
discoveries, are, however, incessantly obtruding themselves upon the world. Ten years now almost count as a
hundred in improvement, and the seventy or eighty
years of a man's life teem with as many new and unex-
pected events, as we have reason to think distinguished
the seven or eight hundred years of the antediluvians.

Here in the America of the dying 1960's and the dawn-
ing 1970's, where the accelerated pace of rapid change
sometimes excites the reaction and backlash of a dark
pessimism, it may be hard to recapture the optimism of
the fathers. But unless we can intuit ourselves into it, at

---

[3]*Memoirs of A. Campbell*, I, 465-66.

least for an hour or so, we cannot hope to understand them.

So much for the general attitude of triumphant hope with which they turned their faces to the frontiers of the new world. Let us look now at some of the particular expressions of that pioneering optimism.

UTOPIANISM

Edwin Scott Gaustad characterizes the freedom of the American frontier spirit in the early nineteenth century under four headings: Utopianism, Transcendentalism, Methodism, and Revivalism. All of these, with the possible exception of Transcendentalism, figured in the rise and development of the Disciples. It is quite interesting, in fact, that Gaustad discusses the Disciples of Christ under the heading of Utopianism, quoting, as he does so, from *The Declaration and Address:* "Dearly beloved brethren, why should we deem it a thing incredible that the Church of Christ, in this highly favored country, should resume that original unity, peace, and purity which belong to its constitution and constitute its glory?"[4] This utopian dream of a united Christendom, if it were utopian, was "the polar star" of Christians and Disciples alike, but one may doubt if it could have been seen in the northern sky except from the vantage ground of the American continent. Many factors combined to make it the star to steer by. One of these was the disestablishment of state churches. Our Pilgrim fathers did not bring this notion with them in the cargoes of their sailing vessels. They came to it slowly and painfully in the new setting. Although Thomas Jefferson's "Bill for Establishing Religious Freedom" passed the Virginia Assembly in 1779, and the First Amendment of the Constitution of the

---

[4]Gaustad, *op. cit.*, p. 139.

United States prohibited the federal establishment of religion, both Connecticut and Massachusetts had been
founded as theocracies, and they continued as such well
into the nineteenth century. The special privileges of the
Puritans before their state laws seemed so deeply en-
trenched in these two New England states that John
Adams "observed that one might as well expect a change
in the solar system as an alteration in the Congregational
establishment."[5] Nevertheless, it did come—to Connecticut in 1818 and to Massachusetts in 1833. And, of course,
it prevailed quite generally on the frontier where our Disciple fathers settled.

Disestablishment gave equal opportunity to all the
sects and denominations of Europe and set the stage for
the furious ecclesiastical warfare which so scandalized the
sensitive spirits of Thomas Campbell and Barton Stone.
One must remember, however, that the war of the denominations was counterbalanced by the freedom, fraternity, and equality of the frontier in most areas of their
life together. Life was fluid and open. And the Disciples
were not the only people who felt driven by the fraternity
of a new social order to seek fraternal bonds within religion. There was something incongruous about an old, divided church in a new United States. It was no accident,
therefore, when the Congregationalists and the Presbyterians joined in a plan of union the same year as the
Cane Ridge Revival (1801), pooling their missionary
moneys for the winning of the West. And it was in accord
with the same quest for a single Christian voice that
the American Bible Society came into existence in 1816,
the American Sunday School Union in 1824, and the
American Tract Society in 1825.

The Disciple approach to the urge toward unity was,

---
[5]*Ibid.*, p. 128.

of course, unique. The federal union of sovereign denominations would not have satisfied them. God's realm was not a republic, but a kingdom—a constitutional monarchy with God himself as king. And the union of Christians required not federation but imperial conquest. Thus it came about that although the goal was union and Christian fraternity, the means was the restoration of the primitive church, and the strategy was often that of debate and controversy. In their own eyes our early preachers were the bearers of the peace and unity of the churches, but in the eyes of denominational churchmen they more often appeared to be proselyters conducting commando raids upon the faithful—men of war, not men of peace. Nevertheless, their single goal was the union of all Christians, and they pursued it with energy that could have sprung up only from the fertile, new ground of the New World.

With unity as the goal, restorationism the means, the Disciples succeeded so well in the second half of the nineteenth century that their utopian vision persisted scarcely dimmed into the early decade of the present century. From 1860 until 1875—only fifteen years—the membership of the young movement grew from 191,000 to 400,000. This was impressive. But the leap of the next twenty-five years was spectacular: from 400,000 to 1,120,-000. All of this came into fitting public recognition when a Disciple, James A. Garfield, was elected to the Presidency and on September 19, 1881, joined Abraham Lincoln in the immortality of martyrdom.

Much of this bursting energy was undisciplined. Disciples had been and continued to be argumentative champions for their plea; at the drop of a hat they challenged members of the denominations to oral and newspaper debate and frequently dueled with them, *in absentia,* from their pulpits. Nevertheless, to put it mildly, Disciples were infused with pioneering zeal and utopian hope. Not for many decades did they contemplate cooperation or mergers with other religious bodies; they were planning to conquer them. As reported by W. C. Morro in his intimate portrait of John W. McGarvey:

They believed in Christian union but they expected it to come by the way of conquest and absorption, not by federation and alliance. In the year 1907, the state convention [of Kentucky Christian Churches] was held at Latonia. A new Roman Catholic church was being constructed near the site of the convention. One day McGarvey stood across the street watching the construction, when some one approached him and asked what he was thinking. His answer was, "I was thinking of the day when that will be one of our churches."[6]

Such was the force and persuasiveness of this restorationist dream that J. W. McGarvey went to his death four years later at the age of 83, apparently never doubting it. In this connection, it is a matter of some surprise to discover that the first anthology of Disciple sermons, *The Living Pulpit of the Christian Church* published in 1868, contains not a single sermon on Christian unity.[7] Not only that, a quick reading discloses only one single, slight allusion to it. The union of Christians was still their port of call, but they were so busy with the navigational chores on the good ship Restoration that they preferred to assume that they were on the right course and that they would arrive ere long at the desired haven.

One of the characteristics of the early nineteenth century, under the influence of utopian dreams, was the development of colonies. The Shakers, who reached a peak strength of about 6,000 members before the Civil War, set themselves up in nineteen colonies in New England,

---

[6]W. C. Morro, *Brother McGarvey: The Life of President J. W. McGarvey of The College of the Bible* (St. Louis: Bethany Press, 1940), p. 120.
[7]W. T. Moore (ed.), *The Living Pulpit of the Christian Church* (Cincinnati: R. W. Carroll & Co., 1868).

New York, Ohio, Indiana, and Kentucky where they practiced strict separation of the sexes, community of property, farming and industry, and a ritual of song and dance not unlike that of the Chasidic Jews. One of these "Shakertowns" is located about twenty miles from Lexington at Pleasant Hill near Harrodsburg, Kentucky; it has recently been restored and is now run as a tourist attraction by its own historical society.

We are more familiar with the Mormons, who, as regards marriage, moved away from Shaker celibacy to polygamy, but from much the same motives—a perfect obedience to Christ "in the latter days." John Humphrey Noyes' Oneida community in western New York, practicing "complex marriage" without permanent unions between couples but with mutual respect of both sexes, was a middle road in a "world looking for a revolution."[8] Some of the same ferment was at work in Robert Owen's effort to establish an ideal, communal society at New Harmony, Indiana, in 1826 without the sanctions and symbols of orthodox belief. Alexander Campbell later tagged Owen and his kind "Bastard Millennarians."[9]

The urge to build up a colony was not without its appeal to the early Disciples. We may tend to forget it or gloss it over, but Campbell and his followers at Brush Run held a meeting on April 13, 1814, at which they appointed a committee to explore the country west of the Ohio River for a suitable location to which to migrate as a body. A committee of five members, of which Alexander Campbell was one, immediately visited "a considerable portion of Ohio" and returned to recommend "the vicinity of Zanesville, Ohio." By unanimous vote of the Brush Run church it was decided on June 8, 1814, that the migration would take place "as soon as they could indi-

---

[8]Gaustad, p. 134.
[9]*Millennial Harbinger,* 1856, p. 698.

vidually make the necessary arrangements."[10] Except for
John Brown's intervention with his gift of his farm and
mansion to his son-in-law, the migration and colonization
would undoubtedly have taken place. If it had occurred
it would have been fully in keeping with what was then
happening under the spell of the American dream and
the lure of new lands to the west.

MILLENARIANISM

By far the most interesting and significant form of the
utopian dream, however, was that which took shape
under the influence of the biblical symbol of the Millennium. The appeal of this symbol to our early leaders can
scarcely be overestimated. In this they were not unique.
The notion that the thousand-year reign of Christ was
near at hand was very widespread among American
Christians in the 1820's, 30's, and 40's—indeed, up to
the period of the Civil War. And it caused an excited
anticipation almost beyond present comprehension. It was
in many ways the pietistic, Protestant form of the American dream in a period when everything was fluid and all
things seemed possible.

Over the pen name of "Philip" Walter Scott published
two articles on "The Millennium" in the July and September issues of *The Christian Baptist* of 1826. In the first of
the articles he wrote:

> Mankind are certainly moving in the horizon of some
> great and eventful change, into the centre of which all
> society must inevitably and speedily be carried. The
> world is in strange commotion; expectation is all aroused
> —anticipation of something good, splendid and unknown,
> is becoming undoubting and impatient, even to painful-
> ness. . . .

---

[10]R. Richardson, *Memoirs of A. Campbell,* I, 460-61.

The time is certainly arrived, when the great political establishments, the powers and principalities of the world . . . must be speedily dissolved; and when the economy of God, which shall be more in unison with the religion of his son and with nature, shall suddenly make its appearance.

Within a year Scott's interest in the Millennium had grown to such importance for him that he drew up plans and published a prospectus for a monthly magazine to be called *The Millennial Herald.* Had not Alexander Campbell carried him away to the Mahoning Baptist Association in August of 1827, where the editor in Scott was submerged for the time being in Scott the evangelist, *The Millennial Herald* would undoubtedly have made its appearance that same autumn.

Alexander Campbell's use of the same symbol in 1830 in the name of his new magazine, *The Millennial Harbinger,* has to be understood against the same popular background. As the Mahoning evangelist, Scott did not lose his interest in the topic. His companion, William Hayden, was not surprised to find him one day in New Lisbon at the home of Mrs. Jacob Campbell talking ecstatically of the Millennium. "Brother Scott and I have just been contemplating how joyful it will be to be in the Millennium—mortals and immortals dwelling together!" said Mrs. Campbell in greeting Hayden, who then listened while Scott launched into an ecstatic survey of millennial prophecies in Ezekiel and Isaiah. That such themes also engaged Scott while preaching can scarcely be doubted.

In the year 1840, William Miller of upstate New York published a book: *Evidence from Scripture and History of Second Coming of Christ About the Year 1843.*[11] Were

---

[11]Gaustad, *op. cit.,* p. 152.

such a man to begin writing and lecturing now the over-
whelming majority of the people in and out of church
would dismiss him as "some kind of a nut." The atmosphere of the 1840's was altogether more friendly. There
is perhaps some gauge to Miller's popular appeal in a few
isolated facts: A whole new crop of papers and magazines
began to tumble from the presses. *The Signs of the Times,*
The Midnight Cry, The Faithful Watchman, The Phila-
delphia Alarm and *The Second Advent of Christ* were
among them.[12] Alexander Campbell, who confessed that
he believed in a literal fulfillment of biblical prophecies
concerning the Millennium, thought enough of the general
excitement to write and publish a series of twenty-six
articles on "The Coming of the Lord" which ran through
the issues of 1841, 1842, and 1843. The *Harbinger* editor
read the books and magazines thrown up by the general
excitement and these he reviewed, quoted or digested in
his magazine, endeavoring to report upon the movement
in all its variety and contradiction, as well as to comment
pro and *con* editorially.

One of Campbell's junior editors, Robert Milligan, was
more than a little captured by millenarianism. During
the years 1856 and 1857 he published twenty articles on
"Prophecy" which dealt with the topic of the Millennium
exegetically, historically, and even chronologically—not always with the enthusiastic support of his senior editor. As
a matter of fact, in the *Harbinger* for April, 1856, on a
page facing Milligan's fifth article, Campbell said, " . . .
although disquisitions on the prophecies, of much re-
spectability, have appeared, and may again appear, on the
pages of the *Millennial Harbinger,* I wish my readers to
understand that I do not endorse any of them."[13]

---

[12]*Millennial Harbinger,* 1843, p. 263.
[13]*Millennial Harbinger,* 1856, p. 188.

He owed it to his readers, he went on to say, to give them "both sides, even diverse theories on such great questions," but the appearance of such views in his magazine implied neither endorsement nor repudiation of any one view. Clearly, he thought the subject highly important; and he did hold decided views of his own regarding it. (Of these, more later.) Campbell did publish five more articles on the "Millennium" over his own initials in 1856.

Before a brief exposition of Campbell's own views, I want to look more closely at those of his junior editor, Robert Milligan, in the series just alluded to. He was later to incorporate the gist of these into his book, *The Scheme of Redemption*. On the general characteristics of the Millennium, he wrote: " . . . during that golden age . . . the knowledge of the Lord will cover the whole Earth, as the waters cover the sea; . . . the Holy Spirit will then be more abundantly poured out on all the churches of the saints; and consequently, . . . 'love, joy, peace, long-suffering, gentleness, goodness, fidelity, meekness and temperance,' will everywhere prevail over the works of the flesh."[14]

Before this happy consummation can be realized, however, there must be "a great and decisive conflict" in which Mohammedanism in the shape of the Ottoman Empire will be overthrown. This event will happen "within the next thirty-six years, or before the epoch of 1892." It could happen much sooner. . . . "The signs of the times clearly indicate this: and the apostolic visions of St. John seem to reveal the near approach of this next event in the order of prophecy. The most eminent theological writers concede that the pouring out of the seven vials of the wrath of God upon the earth is symbolical of the execution of God's righteous judgments on all the enemies of the church; that the first five of these have

---

[14]*Millennial Harbinger*, 1857, p. 361.

been emptied; and that the pouring out of the sixth refers to the final ruin of the Ottoman Empire, which cannot, therefore, be very remote."[15]

Milligan's enthusiasm sweeps him relentlessly to a full chronology. Writing on July 1, 1857, he predicted:

And hence, it follows, if our premises are correct, that in about thirty-five years from this time, the Jews will return to Palestine; that in sixty-five years, they will become converts of Christianity; that in one hundred years they will with the blessing of God and the co-operation of Gentile believers, carry the victories of the cross to the remotest parts of the Earth, and introduce the golden period of the Messiah's reign.[16]

To give these predictions exact dates, the overthrow of the Ottoman Empire and the return of the Jews to Palestine were to have come in 1892, the conversion of the Jews to Christianity in 1922, and the beginning of the Millennium itself in 1967.[17]

Alexander Campbell's interest in all of this was more than casual. In "The Coming of the Lord—No. IX" he wrote, "The subject is daily assuming more interest [1841]. That the coming of the Lord is near, comparatively very near, is now a popular doctrine."[18]

In "No. XXI" of the same series, February, 1843, he wrote:

Although we did not expect that our title of *Millennial Harbinger* was to be so literally and exactly coincident with the facts of an immediate Millennium, as some of our brethren, and all of the Millerite school, would have us think; still I expected, as I yet expect, a Millennium—a thousand years of triumphant Christianity, and at no very distant day.[19]

---

[15]*Millennial Harbinger,* 1856, p. 431.
[16]*Millennial Harbinger,* 1857, p. 430.
[17]*Ibid.*
[18]*Millennial Harbinger,* 1841, p. 424.
[19]*Millennial Harbinger,* 1843, pp. 73-74.

Nevertheless, Campbell's views were considerably at variance with Miller's, as with Milligan's at a later date, indeed, with the whole pre-Millenarian school. Miller held that the world would be 6000 years old in September, 1843. He held that sometime between March 21, 1843, and March 21, 1844, Christ would return, the last judgment would occur, the world would be renewed after a great conflagration and the Millennium—360 millions of ages—would begin.[20] To this Campbell replied with several objections: A Millennium meant what it said—a thousand years. Christ would return at the end of this 1000 years, not at its beginning. Before it could come five radical changes in the religious constitution of society had to occur. These were (1) the conversion of the Jews, (2) the downfall of the Papacy, (3) the overthrow of Mohammedanism, (4) the downfall of Paganism, and (5) the triumph of Christianity.[21] If Miller and his followers thought all this could happen in two years or less, they must have taken leave of their senses. Campbell looked forward to the Millennium, which he saw as "the world's sabbatical." "We have had six Millenniums of the triumph of infidelity, impiety, atheism almost completed; we have the promise of one Millennium of the same endurance, in which the gospel and its friends shall have the Ascendancy."[22] Nevertheless, the thousand years of Christian Ascendancy must not be confused with "eternal life and glory in an eternal inheritance." Heaven and the Millennium are not identical terms. The Millennium is "not the ultimate and eternal state of the church," but is an intermediate period of a thousand years between the king-

---

[20]Gaustad, op. cit., pp. 151-152; Millennial Harbinger, 1841, p. 197.
[21]Millennial Harbinger, 1841, p. 98.
[22]Millennial Harbinger, 1841, p. 196.

doms of this world and the final kingdom of our Lord and his Christ.[23]

Campbell was not above a little joke at William Miller's expense. In the January issue of the *Millennial Harbinger*, 1841, when Miller's prediction was within about two years of fulfillment, Campbell printed a short footnote: "I know it is difficult for those who believe the theory to act in a manner consistent with it. Even Mr. Miller himself, of whose moral excellence I have a good report from various sources, has secured the copyright of his book for some ten years after the end of the world, as if such a right could secure it against the general conflagration!"[24]

One reason why Campbell could throw himself with such energy into "the Reformation of the Nineteenth Century" was his belief, not only that the Millennium was near, but that the reformation of the church was the best means of ushering it in. The reformation of Christianity and the conversion of the world were required, and these depended in no small degree upon human agency. His views called for a more gradual amelioration of society, as is clear from a section of a paragraph in the *Harbinger* in January, 1842:

> Nothing can be more exhilarating than the thought that within the short period of two years from this date, all our misfortunes, cares, vexations, sins, sorrows, and afflictions will be ever past; that we shall witness the destruction of one world and the creation of another; and that we shall see the whole family of God redeemed from the grave, surrounding the throne of God and the Lamb! Who would not desire that such a consummation was just at the door! On that hypothesis, there are myriads of us who would never die—millions that will never be laid in the grave. In a moment, in the twinkling of an eye we shall be present with the Lord, transformed and

---

[23]*Ibid.*
[24]*Millennial Harbinger*, 1841, p. 11.

converted into immortal men. This, indeed, would be an everlasting gospel. *We have occasion only to regret that the evidence on which it is proposed to us is, in our esteem insufficient. But perhaps, we may be somewhat biased in favor of a more extended conversion of the world to Christ than this view warrants. . . .*[25]

Sixteen years later, when a reawakening of religious interest led some Washington, D. C., clergymen to conclude that the end of the world was imminent, Campbell wrote: "Why, it was but yesterday that the mariner's compass was discovered. . . . Still more than all, far off in the East, 'in the climes of the Sun,' there are races, nations and tribes, upon whom the light of truth, science, or even semi-barbarism, has never dawned. There are the countless millions of Chinese, Japanese, Tartars, all the dusky swarms and hordes of the mountains and plains of Eastern Europe. Asia and Africa yet almost unknown to us. . . .

"To say, then, that because we are in the midst of a great religious revival among those who have sat under the drippings of the Sanctuaries of an enlightened land all their days, that the world is to be hurried off the stage, as it were . . . is, it seems to us, to presume beyond all warrants of nature, revelation or science.

"We have too much faith in progress—in, if you will, the foreordained destiny, yet in store, not only for our own, but for other races, to subscribe to the doctrines of these theological gentlemen who hint the last days are at hand."[26]

He had spoken almost a last word on his own position toward the end of 1856 when he wrote, "Prophecies cannot be interpreted *a priori,* or, from what has been, we cannot infallibly in all cases, learn what must hereafter be.

---

[25]*Millennial Harbinger,* 1842, pp. 44-45. Italics mine.
[26]*Millennial Harbinger,* 1858, pp. 335-336.

Modesty sits most gracefully on oneirocritics and interpreters of prophecy."[27]

This last word agrees fundamentally with his first, as published in the "Prospectus" of the *Millennial Harbinger* in January of 1830:

> This work shall be devoted to the destruction of Sectarianism, Infidelity, and Antichristian doctrine and practice. It shall have for its object the development, and the introduction of that political and religious order of society called the MILLENNIUM, which will be the consummation of that ultimate amelioration of society proposed in the Christian Scriptures.[28]

From this brief survey of Disciple Millenarianism it should be clear that preaching in the early period was conducted under the spell of a vision: The church would be reformed, preliminary to the conversion of the world, and the transformation of society. These men felt themselves to be working on the threshold of a glorious new age, the culmination of human progress and the fulfillment of the promises of God. And they thought of themselves, not as spectators to these events, but as actors in its drama, even as agents of God's kingdom on earth. The sense of urgency and expectancy that infused such preaching was tremendous. We can be grateful that Alexander Campbell's moderation and his insistence upon an open mind and free inquiry saved us from the worst abuses of premillenarian speculations to which some of his followers were addicted. Nevertheless, we must never forget that Campbell and the others with him believed literally and profoundly in the imminent triumph of Christianity and its thousand years of earthly dominion.

In no preacher of the Disciples do we find more of

---

[27]*Millennial Harbinger*, 1856, p. 698. An *oneirocritic* is "an interpreter of dreams."

[28]*Millennial Harbinger*, 1830, p. 1.

this sense of urgency and destiny than in Walter Scott, the number-one frontier evangelist of the whole movement. Covering the Western Reserve on horseback, he soon acquired a reputation as a hard rider. To quote my own biography of Scott: "Over a road, through a wood, along a forest path, he thrust his galloping horse. The pulsebeat in his throat kept time with the thudding hoofbeat, and the hurrying tempo became the rhythm of a singing 'Hallelujah Chorus' within him. Mantled in his cloak, . . . he hurried from place to place to tell the news. When someone remonstrated with him for being such a rapid rider, he replied, 'The King's business requires haste.' "[29]

David Edwin Harrell, Jr., who has researched this period thoroughly, enables us to see that the premillennial excitement was shared by Barton Warren Stone, whose magazine in the early 1840's was "crowded with premillennialist material."[30]

The failure of the Millerite philosophies in 1844 was crushing to Walter Scott and so disillusioning to Barton Stone that he closed the pages of *The Christian Messenger* to further discussion of the topic.[31] Scott, after a time, recovered his enthusiasm for the subject, but meantime he moved on to postmillennialist views. These are most fully reflected in a book which he published in 1859: *The Messiahship, or Great Demonstration*.[32] Scott wrote in a

---

[29]Stevenson, *Walter Scott, op. cit.,* pp. 81-82.

[30]David Edwin Harrell, Jr., *Quest for a Christian America: The Disciples of Christ and American Society to 1866* (Nashville: The Disciples of Christ Historical Society, 1966), p. 43. See also *Christian Messenger,* XII (May, 1842), p. 218.

[31]Harrell, *op. cit.,* and *Christian Messenger,* XIV (November, 1844), p. 216.

[32]The full title is *The Messiahship, or Great Demonstration, written for the Union of Christians, on Christian principles, as Plead for in the Current Reformation* (Cincinnati: Bosworth, Chase & Hall, n.d.).

lyrical vein of the United States as "the first of the Messianic nations" predicted in prophecy.[33] In America we have "a new world, a new people, a new government, and in Washington a new hero. Can the symbols and imagery of the prophets then ever be more literally realized?"[34] Something like a benevolent contagion was at work among the nations. In a burst of confidence, not untouched by Anglo-Saxon pride, Scott saw England and America leading the world to the gradual realization of the kingdom of God on earth. "In Great Britain and the United States we have before us, one in the new and one in the old world, the most illustrious proofs that the Messiah who was to come is come, and that the better order of things indicated in the prophets is inaugurated in these two governments at least."[35]

As a result of the Anglo-Saxon example, in God's providence, "nation after nation will be brought . . . to see and appreciate their own rights and freedom, and so understanding the relations of good government and the true religion . . . will take their position among the other nations of the earth that fear and follow God, and consequently ascend from the abyss of wretchedness into which their huge Apostacy from God has plunged them, till at last the whole human family shall participate in the blessings of a christian civilization."[36]

Scott's views had come around to those of Campbell— to a belief in the introduction of the Millennium by the road of human progress. "'The Millennium,' must belong to the history of human progress, and be of gradual introduction. He [the reader] will see that it is not an age to drop down from heaven, but a period of light,

[33]*Ibid.*, pp. 313, 335.
[34]*Ibid.*, p. 298.
[35]*Ibid.*, p. 298.
[36]*Ibid.*, p. 334.

religion, and enjoyment to arise out of the natural and gradual processes of society."[37]

The Messiahship, or Great Demonstration was scarcely off the presses before the country was in the throes of civil strife. The crisis, for Scott, was abysmal. It not only involved his beloved America but seemed thereby to threaten the whole progress of the kingdom of God on earth. In the closing months of 1860 when he was well enough to attend church (at Mays Lick, Kentucky) he refused Communion. "What could Communion mean when Christian brothers were refusing to be bound into one body within the nation? Only once did he respond when asked to speak. That was on January 27, 1861. Then he addressed a few broken remarks on the state of the Union, asked the brethren and sisters to pray for their country, and sat down."[38] Fort Sumter fell April 13. Only ten days later Walter Scott was dead.[39] The doctor's diagnosis was "typhoid pneumonia," but that, surely, was only a symptom. The real cause must have been a broken heart.

REVIVALISM

"Many viewed the Millennium . . . as the climax of the American dream," says Gaustad. "With a little more repentance, a little more reform, with greater piety and morality, the nation might enter that new and glorious, God-ruled age."[40] Thus Millenarianism came to be connected to an older movement, revivalism. That is our next topic. Evangelist Charles G. Finney wrote in the year 1835: "If the church will do her duty the Millennium may come in this country in three years."[41]

---

[37]*Ibid.*, p. 335.
[38]Stevenson, *Walter Scott*, p. 220.
[39]*Ibid.*, p. 223.
[40]Gaustad, *op. cit.*, p. 151.
[41]*Ibid.*

I do not claim that mass revivals were manufactured and copyrighted in America as an exclusive product of the New World. Wesley and Whitefield were preaching to great crowds in the fields of England before Jonathan Edwards was holding cringing sinners over the flames of hell in New England. But conditions were right in America for the fluorescence of revivalism which led to its development and spread on a scale as vast as the new continent.

Some of the ingredients entering into revivalism are easily detected: The disestablishment of state churches, forcing the churches to recruit their members in open competition rather than to receive them from the census bureau of the state; rapid geographical expansion, with fluid and disappearing parish lines and with a population flowing west, outdistancing a college-trained ministry; "a rootless, sprawling society" on a fluid frontier close to death, disease and ambush, scattered in tiny settlements, hungry for companionship, and devoid of grand public buildings and the outward show of civilization. Add to this the low ebb tide of church membership following the Revolutionary War when only about 10 percent of the population were confessed Christians. Add, still further, the lawlessness and roistering immorality likely to grow up on a rootless frontier.

Still you do not explain it, and more especially you do not explain the vividness of the supernatural world or the closeness and terror of hell, upon which revivalistic fervor was so clearly dependent. Perhaps death could not be so easily hidden behind quiet mortuary walls, or cosmeticized and repressed as now; and, as death was in the open, real and close, so also was the hereafter. If one should ask how belief in a golden age shortly to dawn in this world could take on such an otherworldly cast, he should remember that it was no fair and tranquil vision of a placid transition, but an apocalyptic hope, and that heaven hovered low over earthly terrain, while hell bubbled in molten fury under a thin crust just beneath the surface. The other world poised on the brink of a terrestrial invasion. At any rate, the climate and soil of America were ready to receive and encourage revivalism, for it flourished here, and we Disciples were a part of it.

The "Christian" wing of our movement under Barton W. Stone had its beginning in The Great Revival which peaked at Cane Ridge, Kentucky, in August, 1801. The description of James Finley, an eyewitness, fairly sizzles with excitement:

> We arrived upon the ground, and here a scene presented itself, to my mind not only novel and unaccountable, but awful beyond description. A vast crowd, supposed by some to have amounted to twenty-five thousand, was collected together. The noise was like the roar of Niagara. The vast sea of human beings seemed to be agitated as if by a storm. I counted seven ministers, all preaching at one time, some on stumps, others in wagons, and one—the Rev. William Burke, now of Cincinnati—was standing on a tree which had, in falling, lodged against another. Some of the people were singing, others praying, some crying for mercy in piteous accents, while others were shouting most vociferously. While witnessing these scenes, a peculiarly strange sensation, such as I had never felt before, came over me. My heart beat tumultuously, my knees trembled, my lip quivered, and I felt as though I must fall to the ground. A strange supernatural power seemed to pervade the entire mass of mind there collected. I became so weak and powerless that I found it necessary to sit down. Soon after I left and went into the woods, and there I strove to rally and man up my courage. I tried to philosophize in regard to these wonderful exhibitions, resolving them into mere sympathetic excitement—a kind of religious enthusiasm inspired by songs and eloquent harangues. My pride was wounded, for I had supposed that my mental and physical strength and vigor could most successfully resist these influences.

After some time I returned to the scene of excitement, the waves of which, if possible, had risen still higher. The same awfulness of feeling came over me. I stepped upon a log, where I could have a better view of the surging sea of humanity. The scene that then presented itself to my mind was indescribable. At one time I saw at least five hundred swept down in a moment, as if a battery of a thousand guns had been opened upon them, and then immediately followed shrieks and shouts that rent the very heavens. My hair rose upon my head, my whole frame trembled, the blood ran cold in my veins, and I fled for the woods a second time and wished I had stayed at home.[42]

After Cane Ridge, camp meetings became a regular feature of frontier religion. People converged in multitudes on a meeting place from great distances by wagon, horseback, and on foot, equipped with provisions to camp in the open until supplies gave out. There were, of course, no inns or hotels to accommodate such crowds, and no settlements large enough to take them in as private guests. Church historian William Warren Sweet tells us that the Methodists alone had 400 such camp meetings by 1811 and that only nine years later there were a thousand.

Stone's magazine, *The Christian Messenger,* usually carried a section of news headlined, "Revivals." Several of these report or announce camp meetings. Here are two from the year 1827: "We, the Elders and Brethren present, do agree to hold, annually, in Deer Creek District, a union meeting. . . . We design camping on the ground, and request brethren to come prepared for it, with tent and provisions."[43] "On Friday preceding the fifth Lord's day in September next, our Christian Conference will commence at Big Spring, in Overton County, Western

---

[42]F. R. Webber, *A History of Preaching in Britain and America,* Part Three (Milwaukee: Northwestern Publishing House, 1957), pp. 179-180.
[43]*The Christian Messenger,* Vol. 1, No. 7, p. 167.

Tennessee, four miles north of Monroe, . . . and is expected to continue five or six days. We hope the brethren and friends, who live within a reasonable distance, will come prepared with provisions, to camp on the ground. . . ."[44]

Here is a report from September of 1829 from Elder James E. Matthews of Lauderdale, Alabama:

> Our Camp-meeting terminated about 10 days ago. As I had expected, we had a glorious time. . . . The communion on Lord's day evening, exceeded any thing of the kind that I had ever seen. It looked more like Heaven than any thing that I have ever seen before. To see the lovers of Jesus of different denominations, in sweet union, filling two rows of seats, at least fifty yards long; to hear bursts of rapture from several hundred souls, and unceasing shouts of praise for sometime, ascending from the overflowing hearts of christians, of different names, reminded me of the time when 'the wilderness and the solitary place shall be made glad, and the desert shall blossom as the rose.'[45]

James G. Mitchell wrote Editor Stone, September 7, 1830: "I got home yesterday from a tour of 7 weeks travel through Guernsey, Morgan, Athens, Meigs, Muskingum, and Belmont counties. . . .We held two big meetings a week. Some lasting three days. Our congregations were large; frequently a thousand people would attend on Lord's day."[46]

The camp meeting was, of course, the most protracted and the most dramatic form of revival, but that was only one of its manifestations. Meeting places were various— groves, barns, schoolhouses, private dwellings, sometimes church houses. Evangelists moved from place to place. Meetings were held daily, and several times daily. A

---

[44]*Ibid.*, Vol. 1, No. 9, p. 216.
[45]*Ibid.*, Vol. 4, p. 16.
[46]*Ibid.*, Vol. 4, p. 255.

typical day from Walter Scott's busy schedule as Mahoning Evangelist might see him in a schoolhouse in the morning, preaching from a wagon bed in a grove in the afternoon, in a church house at night, after which some of his hearers might trail him to the private house, where he was guest, and stay to hear him out until midnight. Often baptisms by torchlight in the wee hours of the morning followed these nocturnal sessions.[47] Congregations were, perhaps, more often small than large. And churches which came to birth out of these meetings, as they did, were tiny fellowships of fifteen, twenty, thirty members—left in the wake of the evangelist to meet in private homes, as often as not. Reports in *The Christian Messenger* often carried notes like these: " . . . we constituted a church of 33 members . . . "[48] "Since I last wrote I have immersed about twenty-three; I have also planted a church near my own residence, of about thirty members, and another of twelve members six miles west of Winchester."[49]

One can see at once that the evangelistic preaching which brought these churches into being must have been very different from the preaching which went on Sunday after Sunday in the tiny congregations after the evangelist had moved on to other fields. Churches were small; pastors were predominantly laymen.

While the Disciples arose within revivalism as a form of the ministry and continued to use it—indeed, as they still do in the "protracted meetings" in rural areas—they early strove to moderate its highly charged emotionalism. In particular, they rejected the then current views of election, the influence of the Holy Spirit in effecting faith, and the agonizing at the mourner's bench and an anxious seat through which assurance of salvation was wrestled

---

[47]Stevenson, *op. cit.*, p. 81.
[48]*The Christian Messenger,* Vol. 1, p. 260.
[49]*The Christian Messenger,* Vol. 4, p. 17.

from the deity in sweat and tears. There is no space in this lecture to look at the special shape of Disciple evangelism. That must be postponed until later. Nevertheless, it is instructive to notice that both Campbell and Stone had something to say about revivalism in its most florid phases. As early as 1833 Stone wrote:

> All must acknowledge that some good results from such revivals; but all must acknowledge that great evil also grows out of them. Those, who under strong affections, believed they were born of God, and who made a public profession of faith, and fell from it, are of all people in the most pitiable situation, seldom do they ever after embrace religion. . . .
>
> After a lapse of a few years, these scenes pass off forgotten, then another similar revival takes place, and similar events succeed. Such revivals are periodical— once in a few years; but of an evanescent nature: like a flash of lightning.[50]

From Stone's comments it is obvious that he was not repudiating evangelism as a continuing activity, but only the mass psychology of revivalistic epidemics which spasmodically swept the frontier. He, like Campbell, objected more to the content of the preaching and to the theology of conversion employed in the meetings than to revivals as a form of ministry. In 1840 Campbell wrote:

> What, then, shall we think of that religion which is the mere offspring of excited feeling—of sympathy with tones, and attitudes, and gestures—of the noise, and tumult, and shoutings of enthusiasm—of the machinery of the mourning bench, the anxious seat, the boisterous interlocutory prayers, intercessions, and exhortations to "get religion on the spot," &c, &c. with which all are conversant who frequent revival meetings in seasons of great excitement.
>
> It generally—very often, indeed, proves itself to be

[50]*The Christian Messenger*, Vol. 7, p. 211.

animal and imaginative: for when the warmth is over—
when the animal powers begin to flag and the pulse is
reduced to a healthy action, it is all cold and dark
within as before . . . and therefore the frequent aposta-
cies, backslidings, and public scandals brought upon the
Christian name. . . .[51]

"Revival" stood for a particular kind of evangelism in
Campbell's eyes. It was for him a pejorative term; and he
repudiated what it stood for:

The machinery of modern revivals is not divine, but
human. It is certainly delusive. They are undoubtedly
deceived who repose the slightest confidence in it. The
spirit of the Crusades is in it—the spirit of fanaticism is in
it—the spirit of delusion is in it. The Spirit of God is not in
it, else he was not in the Apostles, for he taught them no
such schemes—no such means of catching men. This is a
bait which was never put by Christ's fishermen on the
evangelical hook.[52]

Nevertheless, Campbell did favor evangelistic meetings
lasting over several days or weeks. These he called "protracted meetings." In rural Kentucky, at least, they still
go on under that name, though they are less protracted
than they were a hundred years ago. Of his own favored
form of meeting, Campbell wrote:

Still I am favorably prepossessed towards protracted
meetings. To fix the mind for a long time on the subject
of religion, to abandon the business, and care, and per-
plexity, and pleasures of this life for some days in succession, and to turn all our thoughts to religious truth, to
things unseen and eternal, is, in my judgment, sound
wisdom and discretion. But on such occasions the people must be fed with the bread and water of life—with
the word of God—the gospel facts—revelations, precepts,
and promises, and not with dreams, anecdotes, fictions,

---

[51]*Millennial Harbinger*, 1840, pp. 167-168.
[52]*Millennial Harbinger*, 1840, p. 170.

ballads, and unmeaning vociferations. No effort ought ever to be made to raise the feelings, the affections, or the passions beyond the understanding and faith of the hearers.[53]

Was it possible to devise such an evangelism? The existence of the Disciples of Christ as a religious body and, more especially, their phenomenal success in winning converts before 1900, clearly attest to it. Even so, Disciple evangelism when fully developed was a moderation of revivalism, not an abrogation of it. And it was just as integral to the American frontier. The man largely responsible for shaping it was Walter Scott, who fully merits the title of "Frontier Evangelist."

What Scott and the others undertook was as bold as their conception of the new American nation and the kingdom of God on earth. They set out to do nothing less than to win the world for Christ, who would shortly "make all things new." It could scarcely have happened elsewhere than in the New World and otherwise than under the stimulus of New Ground.

---

[53]*Millennial Harbinger*, 1840, p. 168.

III

The Quest
for Biblical Models

Standing on the soil of the New World, our Disciple fathers envisioned a new society. This new society, moreover, was near, very near; and they thought of themselves as its forerunners. However, the new age which they anticipated was not an uncharted novelty. They described it in terms of the ancient biblical symbol of the Millennium, and they found the means to it through the pristine purity of the church in the days of the Apostles. It is as if they were thinking of two golden ages. One lay behind them in the Mediterranean world of Peter and Paul. The other lay before them on the American continent, to be announced by the trumpet of the seventh angel of the Apocalypse. The way to the golden age of the future was by way of the restoration of the golden age of the church from the ancient past.

The way back to "the proclamation of the Ancient Gospel and the restoration of the Ancient Order"[1] was through direct appeal to the Bible, as over against sectarian interpretation and practice, and it was also in terms of the philosophical assumptions of the Enlightenment. In the very first volume of the *Millennial Harbinger* Alexander Campbell called for an honest, open-minded and

---

[1]*Millennial Harbinger,* 1830 *Prospectus,* item No. 8, p. 1.

commonsense way of reading the Bible. This he stated as a principle:

> That as God had spoken to men in their own language, by his Son and by these Apostles, it followed that in order to make his communications worthy of the character of a REVELATION, he must have used our words in the commonly received sense; for to have taken our words and to have appropriated to them a peculiar and hidden meaning, would have been not to enlighten, but to confound the human understanding.[2]

Over against this single revelation through the Bible, said Campbell, "The Clergy represents *three* revelations as necessary—the written word, the physical influence of the Spirit, and the erudition and spiritual understanding of the preachers."[3] Sectarian clergy, he found, had been "imbued with a mystic spirit, and baptized into spiritual meanings and double senses. . . .To affirm that God means what he says, and says what he means, in the usual acceptation of words, is blasphemy against their doctrine of spiritual meanings and mystical faith."[4] Without quite realizing it, sectarian preachers had worked themselves into an absurdity: The learned were no better guides than the illiterate.

> Of what use, then, are the rules of construction, or the literal meaning of words, to the person who relies upon an internal spiritual operation, which is supposed to unveil the secrets of the written Oracle, and to communicate the spiritual meaning of religious hieroglyphics? Hence it is that we hesitate not to place in the same class the most illiterate proclaimer and the most accomplished scholar who believes in a revelation upon a revelation.[5]

---

[2]*Millennial Harbinger*, 1830, p. 558. Original in italics.
[3]*Ibid.*
[4]*Millennial Harbinger*, 1831, pp. 199-200.
[5]*Millennial Harbinger, ibid.*

The resultant confusion in Christendom Campbell likened to the plague of the frogs called upon the Egyptians by Moses in the Exodus:

> Of all the plagues under which christendom has been afflicted for 'a time, and times, and the dividing of a time;' for the last twelve hundred and sixty years, the greatest has been the Egyptian mythological rules of interpretation, in the hands or heads of the 'christian priesthood.' God has given them over to an *undiscerning* mind. The majority have believed a lie. There is not a fountain in the land into which these spiritual frogs have not found their way.[6]

Campbell's "rules of interpretation" were sound. After more than 150 years they stand up well, both to the principles of older hermeneutics and to those of "the New Hermeneutic." By this means Campbell hoped to remove the green, blue, and yellow spectacles with which his contemporaries were reading the Bible and because of which they were in conflict over the real color of the hallowed page. "Thus one professor reads the Bible with John Calvin on his nose, another with John Wesley on his nose, a third with John Gill on his nose, and a fourth with good old Thomas Boston, or the good old lights of Scotland. Thrice happy is the man who lifts the Bible as if it had dropped from heaven into his hand alone, and whose eyes are anointed with the true eye salve that he may see."[7]

What Campbell did not detect was that he himself was wearing spectacles—the rose-colored glasses of Lord Francis Bacon and empiricist John Locke superimposed upon the lenses of John Newton's classical mechanics. It could hardly have been otherwise, for Newton's vision of the universe and Locke's theory of knowledge were so much in the air that anyone breathing them in at that

---

[6]*Millennial Harbinger, ibid.*
[7]*Millennial Harbinger,* 1832, p. 344.

time might easily imagine that they were God's native
atmosphere. W. E. Garrison has shown that the picture of
the universe held by Deists and the more traditional
Christian believers (or "apologists" as he calls them) was
essentially the same picture:

> The universe had suddenly become very simple. God
> had made the world and set it going according to Newton's
> law and had then left it to run. Any further traffic between
> God and the world could be only an invasion of the mun-
> dane sphere by a divine power not normally active in it. The
> apologists believed that such an invasion had occurred in
> the redemptive process; the deists denied it. Any revelation
> of the divine will or of religious truth must come in the
> form of miraculous oral discourse between God and repre-
> sentatives of the human race chosen by him. The orthodox
> believed that such discourse had occurred and that the
> Bible contained a record of it; the deists denied it.
>
> Thus, since their basic patterns of thought were identical,
> Christian apologists became deeply tinged with the hue of
> that against which it was making its defense.[8]

To say this is not to condemn the fathers, for that is
precisely what the theological task of every generation
is—the translation of the Christian tradition through forms
that make contemporary sense in terms of the current
understanding of the world. We can never see more in
the Bible than our contemporary presuppositions will al-
low us to see. One of the reasons why we are having
a hard time developing an acceptable theology of preaching in this latter half of the twentieth century lies precisely here: Our contemporary picture of the universe is
so garbled—fabricated from miscellaneous pieces of Newton's and Einstein's and Darwin's world views wired and
pasted together to resemble a Rube Goldberg invention.
Whether this makes us better or poorer judges of the pre-

---

[8]W. E. Garrison and A. T. DeGroot, *Disciples of Christ: A History* (St.
Louis: Bethany Press, 1948), pp. 56-57.

suppositions of Disciple pioneers, we shall have to admit that theirs were far less complicated and ambiguous than ours, as well as more widely shared by their contemporaries, and that they did derive from them a clear, consistent theology of preaching—which is a great deal more than we have been able to do in our generation.

What the Disciple fathers believed and did about preaching was largely determined by these three factors: (1) Their reaction against the sectarian division with which they clashed in the Protestant denominations around them—which division they attributed to an overlay of creeds, confessions of faith, and ecclesiastical inventions superimposed upon the simple faith and practice of the New Testament church. (2) Their direct appeal to the Bible in anticipation of the actual recovery of the Ancient Gospel and the genuine restoration of the Ancient Order of the church, renewed in purity, in unity, and in power, and through its renewal, renovating the world. (3) The presuppositions of the world view within which they necessarily operated. Turn now to the implications for preaching which arose from these forces:

IMPLICATIONS FOR PREACHING

1. *The rejection of the homiletical essay.* Campbell, Stone and Scott saw little that they approved in the sectarian pulpit. One source of their discontent was the homiletical essay, frequently attached to a short biblical text. The practice had grown up in England under the influence of Tillotson (1630-1693), by whom the sermon was transformed into "a moral essay, the vehicle of a sober, utilitarian, prudential ethic, rather than a proclamation of the Gospel of the Kingdom." So wrote Sydney Smith (1771-1845). He went on to say, "Every man of sense, taking up an English sermon, expects to find it

a tedious essay, full of commonplace morality."[9] Comment-
ing on this development, which he reported, Norwegian
Bishop Brilioth says, "The homiletical essay may of course
be biblical, but more often it is not. At any rate, it rarely
attempts to give a real exposition of a text, but contents
itself with a short biblical quotation as a starting point."[10]

Walter Scott, writing in the *Christian Baptist* for January 5, 1824, poured his scorn upon such preaching:

> The religious public devoutly reckon a pulpit man to be
> explaining this term ["gospel"], and to preach the glad
> tidings of heaven, if he be but deducing some grave spiri-
> tual secret from such scraps of Holy Writ as the following
> —"Naphtali is a hind let loose"—"Ephraim is a cake un-
> turned" — "Remember Lot's wife" — "Judas went and
> hanged himself"—"We took sweet counsel together," &c.,
> &c. Such texts . . . may afford the learned, subtle, and
> seraphic preacher an opportunity of exhibiting his own
> pretty talents before a polite and fashionable assembly. . . .

But Scott regarded them of little worth in proclaiming
the Gospel.

With this sentiment Barton Stone was in hearty accord.
"Apathetic and moral lectures on religion," he said, "have
almost ruined the world, and swelled the number of scep-
tics."[11]

Campbell reserved some of his choicest barbs for
preachers who used texts in this manner. At various times
he called them "scrap doctors,"[12] "flowery and elegant
sermonizers,"[13] "local sermonizing textuaries," "philosoph-

[9]Yngve Brilioth, *Landmarks in the History of Preaching* (London: SPCK,
1950), pp. 32-33. Used by permission of SPCK.

[10]*Ibid.*

[11]Elder James M. Mathes (ed.), *Works—Elder B. W. Stone to which is
added a Few Discourses and Sermons* (Cincinnati: Moore, Wilstach, Keys
& Co., 1859), p. 342.

[12]*Millennial Harbinger,* 1853, p. 547.

[13]*Christian Baptist,* May 5, 1828.

ical, speculative essayists," "fashionable, beautiful and eloquent orators," "gifted and highly accomplished essayists, lecturers, orators, sermonizers."[12]

Such preaching never wanted for sermon topics, but it did little to advance knowledge of the Bible—for preacher or people. Indeed:

> Any person, by the help of a margin Bible or a concordance, with the outlines of some system of theology in his cranium, can make as many sermons as there are verses in the Bible, and deduce many doctrines and notions which never entered into the head or heart of any of the Jewish prophets or christian apostles."[14]

In the light of such views, we are not surprised to learn that Campbell wanted to dismantle the whole edifice of textual preaching as it then was. He found in the Bible no warrant for it. But, more than that, he saw in it a source of *eisigesis*—reading meanings into scripture that were not there and that never would be there.

> The whole system of sermonizing, text preaching, expounding scriptural scraps, and of doctrinal expositions, is unauthorized by God, and is not the way to save sinners or edify saints. There is no trace of such a mode of procedure in the apostolic age, nor in the times immediately subsequent thereto. This system has darkened the counsel of God, and filled the world with error.[15]

This did not mean that a man was forbidden to use a short text in a sermon. It was permissible to do so, but only from the perspective of whole books and the whole written drama of redemption. If a text were used, it should be "approached through a whole epistle, or section of an epistle, or portion of the sacred history; and set before the audience in the light of its own context."[16] In a word,

---

[14]*Christian Baptist*, May 5, 1828.

[15]*Millennial Harbinger*, 1834, p. 589.

[16]*Ibid.*

the only textual preaching to be trusted was contextual preaching.

2. *The Disciple fathers were equally vehement in rejecting homiletical harangue.* Noisy, ranting sermons had considerable entertainment value. Abraham Lincoln even confessed that when he listened to a sermon he wanted it to be delivered by a minister who preached "like a man fighting bees."[17] In this he was not supported by his Disciple contemporaries.

There is a vast difference between emotion and emotionalism. Genuine emotion arises from perception, memory, and imagination and from ideas which are made to live in terms of perception, memory, and imagination. Genuine emotion calls no attention to itself but rather recreates the vivid mental world out of which it sprang and reenforces and ratifies the ideas which called it forth. Emotionalism, on the other hand, arises from biological rhythms, from generalized sentiments, and sentimentalities and prejudices and from crowd contagion. Emotionalism exists not for the sake of ideas and rational actions but for its own sake, or for the sake of some irrational action. It is hypnotic, even orgiastic, in effect. As such it is a highly etherealized form of intoxication, hardly more ennobling than its carnal cousin, alcoholic intoxication. No effective preaching can be done without emotion, but we could well do without emotionalism.

No one was more aware of this nor more entertaining in discussing it than Alexander Campbell. Take for example his satire of what we might call the "Sabbath syndrome" of the young divine who takes himself too seriously:

> My young priest generally assumes a sanctimonious air, a holy gloom overspreads his face, and a pious sedateness reigns from his eyebrows to his chin. His very tone of voice

[17]Edgar DeWitt Jones, *Lincoln and the Preachers* (New York: Harper & Row, 1948), p. 152.

participates of the devotion of his soul. His words flow on with a solemn slowness, and every period ends with a heavenly cadence. There is a kind of angelic demeanor in his gait, and a seraphic sweetness in all his movements. With his Sunday coat, on a Sabbath morn, he puts on a mantle of deeper sanctity, and imperceptibly learns the three grand tones—the sabbath tone, the pulpit tone, and the praying tone—these are the devout, the more devout, and the most devout.[18]

When it comes to pulpit action, especially if he is under the influence of revivalism, the young preacher must work himself up into a fever pitch. Campbell described it this way:

Often I have seen a preacher try to get his mind abroach until he began to snuff the breeze like a whale snorting in the North Atlantic Ocean. It is more easy to bring a 74 gun ship into action in a gale of wind, than to get the mind to bear upon the text, until the nostrils catch the corner of a volume of air, and sneeze it out like a leviathan of the deep. I have seen other preachers who can strike fire no other way than by friction of their hands, and an occasional clap, resembling a peal of distant thunder. In this holy paroxysm of clapping, rubbing, sneezing, and roaring, the mind is fairly on its way, and the tongue in full gallop, which, like a race horse, runs the swifter the less weight it carries. The farther from nature the nearer the skies, some preachers seem to think. But so it is whenever they acquire this habit it is almost incurable. They can neither speak of God nor man in the pulpit to purpose, as they suppose, unless, when, like a boiler of a steam boat, they are almost ready to burst. This is one extreme. There are various degrees marked on the scale before we arrive at this dreadful heat. There is a certain pitch of voice which is at least ten degrees above the natural key. To this most preachers have to come before their ideas get adrift. Their inspiration is kindled from the noise they create.[19]

---

[18]*Christian Baptist*, Jan. 5, 1824.

[19]*Christian Baptist*, "Sermons to Young Preachers—No. I," September 7, 1829.

The effect of such preaching could be like the insistent beat of voodoo drums upon the mesmerized minds of its devotees. Its power over the imagination and revulsion of Alexander Campbell was great enough that one occasion of it lived vividly in his memory for thirty years. Though he did not write about it until 1855, the incident itself, he said, occurred October 7, 1825. He could date it exactly. With mingled amusement and consternation he wrote about a meeting of the Dover Baptist Association addressed by a certain Elder Carr. The excitement stirred up by Elder Carr, though he was a Baptist, was "equal to Wesleyan Methodism in its palmiest days. What a shaking there was in the camp! What a hugging of men with men! What a weeping of females! . . . I thought I had got into a Methodist camp-meeting, and began to apprehend that it would find its way into the preacher's tent. I looked round, and saw the muscles begin to work, in grotesque forms, in the cheeks of Bishop Semple. It spread through our whole tent, with the exception, perhaps, of Elder Broaddus and myself. There we sat in solemn contemplation. I listened, with unusual attention, to ascertain the connection between the ideas of the speaker and the emotions of the hearers; between the sympathies and movements of the congregation and what he said. I began to wish that I, too, could weep, and sought to hear something that might touch my sympathies. But apart from the *action,* the *vociferations,* and the *intonations* of the ascending and descending climax of passion, I could not hear one word, or appreciate one idea, as the worthy parent of what I saw and heard in the great congregation."[20]

Although Barton Stone was always more favorably disposed to revivals and revivalism than Campbell, his views on emotionalism did not greatly differ from those of the

---

[20]*Millennial Harbinger,* 1855, p. 130.

Bethany sage. "A person may also preach with a great vociferous zeal and manner," he said. "This may be and often is nothing more than mere animal nature, without the spirit."[21]

Campbell castigated such a way of preaching. He called it "animalism." "It occasionally roars like a lion and screams like a panther. It seems rather to get into the lungs of the preacher and into his heart, and to reside in his throat rather than his soul." "Every good bruise is an effectual argument." "It converts more persons by an anecdote, a shout, a denunciation; or by the word '*damnation*,' at the top of the voice, or by '*hell-fire*,' uttered in the midst of great animal excitement, than by all the gospel facts or arguments from Genesis to the Apocalypse."[22]

From this vehement rejection of emotionalism one must not be misled to the conclusion that Campbell rejected emotion in preaching. This becomes quite clear, not only from Campbell's own practice, in which he could so captivate his hearers that they lost all sense of time in the pleasure of hearing him, but it also shows specifically right in the midst of his denunciations of "animalism" in the pulpit. Although he called for a pulpit delivery "in the natural tone of voice and in the natural key,"[23] he was fully aware that a preacher, to be effective, had to feel his message to the point of forgetting and losing himself in it. This is evident in a few quotations from "Sermons to Young Preachers—No. II":

> He who speaks to some great, or good, or interesting object, loses himself in his subject; forgets almost his own identity, and sees or feels nothing but that for which he speaks. His object is in his heart and before his eyes con-

---

[21]Mathes (ed.), *Elder Barton W. Stone, op. cit.*, p. 343.

[22]*Millennial Harbinger*, 1843, pp. 462-464.

[23]*Christian Baptist*, September 7, 1829.

tinually. From it he derives his inspiration, his zeal, his eloquence.

The deepest and most moving feelings come, not from aiming at feeling at all, nor from playing upon people for effects, but in forgetting oneself as one becomes completely absorbed in his message.

> When a man feels his subject, he forgets himself. 'Tis then, and then only, he speaks to the heart, and speaks with effect. The understanding is, and must be addressed, that the heart may be taken. For unless the heart or the affections of men are elevated to the admiration and love of God, and fixed upon him, all religion is a name, a pretense, vain, and useless.
>
> In the art of speaking, the great secret is first to form clear conceptions of the subject to be spoken; and then to select such terms as exactly express our conceptions. To do this naturally, is the consummation of the art of speaking. All men can speak intelligibly, and many men fluently, upon the subjects with which they are every day conversant. And if we would make others feel, we must feel ourselves.[24]

3. *Preaching as an act of war against Calvinists and Arminians.* Revulsion against pulpit harangues had deeper roots than matters of taste in etiquette and aesthetics. It lay in a decisive rejection of the theological foundations of revivalistic conversions. As masterfully summarized by Granville Walker in his study, *Preaching in the Thought of Alexander Campbell.*[25] "On the doctrinal side, the mystery and darkness were produced by Calvinist and Arminian dogmas which held that faith came through regeneration by the Holy Spirit, and was therefore inaccessible to man except by the direct interposition of the Spirit. And on the practical side, preaching became the medium by

---

[24]*Christian Baptist,* December 7, 1829.
[25](St. Louis: Bethany Press, 1954), pp. 28-29. Used by permission of Bethany Press.

which this 'mystery' was sustained. For preaching on the frontier had become identified very largely with a system of revivalism which sought to induce the emotional orgies that were regarded as outpourings of the Spirit. Preaching and the conception of faith were inseparable."

Since the Disciple pioneers to a man regarded this conception of faith as a sinful error, they opposed it. In fact, they attacked it in almost every sermon and in their writings. Examples are abundant. Here is one from Barton Stone as he satirizes the error:

> The sinner must have a new revelation to understand the written revelation; or new light to see the old light: therefore the old revelation or light is useless to any until God is pleased to give the new light? This doctrine puts the scriptures in the background indeed! They can no longer be considered the power of God unto salvation—no longer can it be said, "The entrance of thy word giveth light, it giveth understanding to the simple"—no longer can they be considered as the means of life, light and salvation to the world—they answer no better purpose to the unconverted, than a sundial in a cloudy day. . . .[26]

In the March issue of the *Christian Messenger*, 1833, Barton Stone published a skillful subversion, written with tongue in cheek. He entitled it "An Orthodox Sermon." The whole is worth reading, not only as a sample of the satirist's art, but also as an incident in the conflict of dogma then in progress. I do not have space to give a synopsis here, except to say that Stone advanced the orthodox line of hard Calvinism as presented in the Westminster Confession of Faith. At each of the five points of the sermon, he raised objections, which were tossed aside by the preacher as beneath notice or prompted by ignorance or "carnal reason." Not even the objections derived from the plain word of scripture could hold, because the

---

[26]*Christian Messenger*, Vol. 4, p. 80.

surface meaning could not be true. Take, for example, that God loved all men: Logic shows that if God had called all men, he would have called them effectually; therefore, all would obey. But, since not all men do actually obey, God must not have called them, and, if he had not called them, it was because he did not love them; therefore, God must love only the elect.

The force of Stone's attack is nowhere more obvious than in an illustration under the third point, "and those whom he predestined he also called" (Romans 8:30):

> A father had two little children, both born deaf and dumb. They are playing together in his yard. He calls them—they cannot hear; he calls aloud, still they hear not. He is enraged with one for not hearing and obeying him. The other he effectually calls by some secret intimation, and makes willing and obedient. The one he severely punishes—the other he graciously rewards.—This partiality and severity we reprobate and abhor in an earthly father. Can we love the same character in any being—even in God?"[27]

An illustration like that comes out of a theology of preaching which we must presently investigate, but, for the moment, consider the atmosphere of combat within which early Disciple preaching was conducted. It must not be supposed that the ridicule and abuse heaped upon preachers of the sects was unrequited. Moreover, on the rude frontier, verbal attack was not always paid back in kind. Walter Scott reported some of the opposition which he stirred up on the Western Reserve: "In one place where I was baptizing, just as I raised the baptized person up out of the water, I saw a great stick hanging or rather shaking over my head. On another occasion I was interrupted by a person with a sword-cane. At one place they set loose my mare in the night, and at Noblestown in the

---

[27]*Christian Messenger*, Vol. VII, pp. 77-84.

midst of six Presbyterian congregations, the sectarian population cut off all the hair from her tail."[28] In this rough kind of "horseplay," Disciple evangelists could usually give as good as they received. No one did this with more verve and enjoyment than Raccoon John Smith, whose encounters with the Calvinists of Kentucky were almost legendary.

Anyone now reading the sermons in *The Living Pulpit of the Christian Church*[29] may find them so heavily theological and deadly dull that he may wonder how the original hearers ever stayed awake while listening to them. What he has to remember is that these sermons were engagements in a theological warfare and that nothing is more interesting or entertaining than a good fight. Audiences knew the rules of this contest as well as sports fans now know the rules of arena and gridiron. Even when the logomachy was not virulent hand-to-hand encounter, it was always rumbling in the wings. It lent an air of excitement to a Disciple sermon hard for us to imagine.

This spirit of combat was not confined to sermons and their informal aftermath. It was injected into the magazines and erected into forensic occasions of public debate, attendant with the excitement of a football game. Nearly all of the early Disciple preachers engaged in this sort of thing with gusto. They went at their task of proclaiming the gospel like the soldiers of an attacking army who expected to sweep all before them. In this atmosphere of almost universal debate, individual sermons partook not only of the spirit but also of the techniques of argumentation and debate.

It is perhaps for this reason that early Disciples never produced a significant literature of devotion. Robert Richardson's *Communings in the Sanctuary* stands almost

---

[28]*Christian Baptist*, VII, p. 271.
[29]W. T. Moore (ed.) (Cincinnati: W. R. Carroll & Co., 1868).

alone, one slim volume of devotion in a whole library of debate.

Both Campbell and Stone began to witness what they had set in motion as they watched the preaching of lesser disciples. As Granville Walker puts it, "Despite the fact that the *Christian Baptist* and *Millennial Harbinger* were themselves filled with tirades against the sects and errorists of the day, he [Campbell] adjured the preachers of the reformation to leave denunciation out of their proclamations and preach the gospel only."[30]

Writing on "Reformation of the Preachers of Reformation," Campbell took as a text a facetious query of a reader: "Ought not a reformer to treat all the matters at issue between the disciples and the sects with as much levity as possible, and convert the meeting-house into a place of amusement? Ought he not, in order to expose error with the most effect, to act the part of a religious mountebank, and lampoon and ridicule all the *isms* in christendom, in order to prepare the way for the introduction of the ancient faith?"[31] It is evident that the question was not a theoretical exercise, but that it reflected a growing practice of Disciple preachers. Campbell's reply was characteristically spirited. Among other things, he said: "To see a young man who cannot do more than parse a common sentence of the King's English, mount the stand and lampoon all the Rabbis and Doctors, all the commentators and critics of a thousand years, as a set of fools or knaves—as a pack of dunces or mercenary imposters—is infinitely more nauseating than *lobelia* itself, and shockingly repulsive to all the finer feelings of our nature. Again, to see a person, young or old, appear in the garb

---

[30]Walker, *op. cit.*, p. 195. "Articles pleading with the preachers to abandon this unsavory practice begin to appear in quick succession in the *Millennial Harbinger* in 1835."

[31]*Millennial Harbinger*, 1835, p. 134.

of a preacher of righteousness, with the living Oracles in his hand, addressing us in the name of Jesus Christ; with the flippancy of a comedian, courting smiles, instead of wooing souls to Jesus Christ, acting the religious mountebank, full of levity, displaying wit and seeking the reputation of a smart fellow in the presence of God—is the climax of irreverence as respects God, and inhumanity as respects man."[32]

What Campbell himself handled in public debate with such grace and dignity did not always come out so well in his lesser imitators. In that same article, he went on to even severer castigation: "We have heard of some preachers only a little smitten with this disease, who have made the ancient order of things to send forth a more offensive savor than Solomon's dead fly in the ointment of the apothecary."[33]

Clearly, Campbell wanted to put a quietus on the spirit of controversy and debate then abroad in Disciple preaching. All the same, one has to admit that the instrument with which Campbell hoped to put down debate was itself more than a little infused with the spirit and techniques of debate. For some decades to come, Disciple preachers imitated the adviser and ignored the advice.

Barton W. Stone also commented on the blight of the debating spirit. In the public debates themselves he saw little profit. People attending them had usually chosen sides and rooted for their champion like spectators of gladiatorial combat. Few minds were changed. "A few unsophisticated persons may be proselyted to your opinion, but one renewed soul is of more value than a score of such proselytes. . . ."[34]

---

[32]*Millennial Harbinger*, 1835, p. 135.
[33]*Millennial Harbinger*, 1835, p. 136.
[34]Mathes (ed.), *op. cit.*, p. 341.

As for the controversial and debating spirit in the pulpit itself, Stone was decidedly against it: "Seldom do we see in the same person a warrior and an humble, devoted Christian. *Rara avis in terra.* [A rare bird in the earth.] Such acquire a controversial habit and temper. They may proselyte many to their opinions, and greatly increase their numbers; but the children are like the parents, lean and pigmy things."[35]

Although there was much to regret in preaching that participated in the methods and manners of debate, then so popular in America, there is one charge that we cannot lodge against the pulpit of that day which so often applies to our own: Preaching was seldom dull. And preaching was listened to, in this period, not only for its solemn instruction, but because it was such fun. An illustration of that fact is found in Walter Scott's account of an "Excursion to Virginia" in March of 1834. He and thirty-five passengers took cabins in the river steamer *Planter* from Cincinnati to Wheeling. Six of the passengers were clergymen: a Presbyterian, an Episcopalian, a Universalist, a Baptist, a Dutch Reformed (who could not participate because of his imperfect English), and Walter Scott, a Disciple. Let Scott tell it:

> Here we were then, five of us cooped up with nearly thirty more, all as impatient and undoubting on the subject of religion, perhaps, as ourselves! What was to be done? What was to be expected? Any thing but war! Nothing but war. Being somewhat indisposed I had hoped that my debilitated and sunken frame would have been permitted to indulge in ease during our three or four days journey up the river, but no: 'war in the wigwam:' there is no rest here.[36]

---

[35] *Ibid.*, pp. 340-341.
[36] Scott's *Evangelist*, Vol. 3, No. 3, pp. 54-62.

The first night out "for the entertainment of the company"—notice the wording—it was agreed that each of
the five ministers should speak for fifteen minutes on a
topic of his choice. The next night there was another
round of speeches, these to be without time limit. All were
highly theological and, because of the differing creedal
loyalties of the men, highly controversial. By such means,
without radio, television, or even riverboat stage plays, the
passengers whiled away their time and shortened the
long, tedious voyage upriver.[37]

4. *A clear-cut theology of preaching.* We are being
driven by each point in our discussion to a deeper level.
It is now time to consider the fact that the fathers were
compelled in their conflict with revivalism to develop their
own theology of preaching. This they did.

Several years ago the late T. Hassell Bowen, a beloved
colleague, while on sabbatical at Harvard, engaged
theologian Paul Tillich in what turned out to be a typical
Disciple conversation. As Bowen reported it to me, it went
something like this:

Bowen: Professor Tillich, how would you characterize
Christian faith?

Tillich: I think of it as the experience of being grasped.
How do you think of it?

Bowen: As belief in the evidence that Jesus is the
Christ.

In that reply Bowen proved himself to be an orthodox
follower of both Campbells, Walter Scott, and Barton W.
Stone. This view of faith goes clear back to Thomas Campbell, before the writing of the *Declaration and Address.*
In his heresy trial before the Washington Presbytery,
February 9-12, 1808, the first of seven charges lodged
against him asserted that Mr. Campbell denies "that any

---

[37]*Ibid.*

persuasion, or assurance or confidence that we in particular through the grace of our Lord Jesus Christ shall be
saved belongs to the nature of saving faith."[38]

Garrison and DeGroot's explanation of Thomas Campbell's "heretical" position is clear and concise:

> The main point about "saving faith" was that [Thomas]
> Campbell refused to include any sort of mystical or emo-
> tional uplift, interpreted as giving "assurance that Christ is
> *mine*," as an essential element in faith. It may accompany
> a high degree of such faith or it may not. The validity of
> faith does not depend upon it. [Before his judges in the
> Washington Presbytery, Thomas] Campbell stood by his
> position on the nature of faith, as an intelligent response of
> the mind to evidence rather than a Spirit-given emotional
> experience. . . . A witness on behalf of Mr. Campbell testi-
> fied that he "rested completely satisfied with the definition
> of 1 John 5:1, 'Whosoever believeth that Jesus is the Christ,
> is born of God.'" The presbytery voted that this item of
> the libel was "clearly proved."[39]

Alexander Campbell followed faithfully in his father's
steps. To put the matter in the briefest possible compass,
let me point out that Alexander identified "five links in the
chain of salvation." These were: "facts, testimony, faith,
feeling, action—the end of which is salvation."[40]

By *facts* Campbell meant what we have come to call
"God's mighty acts" and "the event of Christ." He meant
God's *deeds* in history for us men and for our salvation.
As explained by Granville Walker, "The gospel facts themselves, and not some external outpouring of the Spirit
[subjectively experienced], were the source of the power
of the Christian faith. Those facts comprised 'all that
is recorded in the sayings and doings of Jesus Christ,
from his birth to his coronation in the heavens.' But they

---

[38]Garrison and DeGroot, *op. cit.*, p. 132.
[39]*Ibid.*, p. 133.
[40]*Millennial Harbinger*, 1845, p. 434.

could be, and were, concentrated into a few events of particular importance which together exhibited all of the love of God in the gift of his Son:"[41]

> He died for our sins, He was buried in our grave, He rose from the dead for our justification, and is ascended to the skies to prepare mansions for his disciples, comprehend the whole, or all the heads of the chapters which narrate the love of God, and display his moral majesty and glory to our view.[42]

This quotation from the *Millennial Harbinger* in 1835 reminds a modern reader of C. H. Dodd's discovery of the kerygmatic pattern in apostolic preaching more than a hundred years later. For Campbell—indeed, for all the Disciple fathers—Christianity had an objective base—it rested not upon subjective human feelings but rather upon what God had done in Christ. These deeds were a matter of record in the Christian scriptures. "The record of the testimony is the object of faith. Hence faith requires testimony, testimony concerning facts, and facts require a witness. The historian records facts."[43]

The meaning of *faith* becomes clear when contrasted with *knowledge* and *opinion*. Campbell put it this way: "I *believe* that Jesus Christ died for our sins, I *know* that the sun gives us light, and I *am of the opinion* that all infants dying shall be saved.

"A person's faith is always bounded by testimony; his knowledge by observation and experience, and his opinions commence where both of these terminate, and may be boundless as God's creation or human invention."[44]

---

[41]Walker, p. 40.

[42]*Millennial Harbinger*, 1835, pp. 340-341, in Walker, *op. cit.*

[43]*The Evidences of Christianity; A Debate between Robert Owen. . .and Alexander Campbell. . . .* (Cincinnati: Bosworth, Chase & Hall, 1871), p. 228.

[44]*Christian Baptist*, Feb. 6, 1826. Italics mine.

A favorite scripture of all the fathers was: "So, then, faith comes by hearing, and hearing by the word of God" (Romans 10:17, A. Campbell's New Testament). It is easy to caricature such a position as "literalistic, legalistic" or even "rationalistic," but it is evident that the fathers were committed to something more dynamic and comprehensive than such labels would imply. Campbell insisted, "If a man really believes any fact, his faith soon becomes apparent by the influence of the fact upon him."[45]

A reader of the *Christian Baptist* asked Editor Campbell in the issue of March 2, 1829, "Do you really believe, that if a man can say simply that he believes the truth of the scriptures, and that they are the word of God—that the salvation of that man is secured to him. . . .?"

To this Campbell replied, "To this query, in the fair import of the terms, I answer positively: No. It is only they 'who keep his commandments, who shall have a right to enter into his heavenly city.' Those whom the Judge of all will address with 'well done,' are those who have done well. No man, either at death, or in the final judgment, will be justified in believing the whole, or any part of scripture; *believing it in any way, historically, or in the popular style*. Men are justified here by faith, and there by works: or in other words, by faith, they are introduced into the state of favor, so that their prayers may be heard, and their works accepted—But the justification here is of pure favor: it is God's own philanthropy which grants them acceptance through faith in his testimony." [Italics mine.]

An earlier exchange between reader and editor in the *Christian Baptist* also sets faith in its full context of Christian life. The reader asked, "How can we be assured that

---

[45]*Christian Baptist*, Apr. 5, 1824.

this work [rebirth] is accomplished in us?" Campbell answered, "Our immersion in the name of the Father, &c. is an act of which we are conscious at the time, and which we can remember; and our spirit is, when renewed by the Spirit of God, also conscious that we love the brethren and love God; and we are assured, as John teaches, that we have passed from death to life when we love the brethren."[46]

Still another question-answer exchange—on December 1, 1828—fairly corrects a literalistic view of preaching as the mere recital of scripture:

"Query: Does preaching the gospel consist in publishing it, as it is found in the Spirit's own words [in the letter of the Bible], or in publishing discourses made by men about it?"

"Answer: The preaching of the gospel never did mean *making sermons or discourses about it,* no more than the cure of diseases has been effected by disquisitions upon pathology or the nature of diseases and remedies; but in the proclamation of the great facts [that is the deeds, the mighty acts of God] found in the historical books of the New Testament, supported by such evidences and arguments as the apostolic testimonies contain and afford."

As for the place of the Holy Spirit—and there is a place!—"The Spirit of God becomes the indwelling guest of Christians as they read, study and search the Scriptures and are obedient to its demands."[47]

5. *The search for biblical models.* Such a theology of preaching, bolstered as it was by restorationist ideals, led naturally to a search for biblical models in preaching. The Bible was read, not only to supply the testimony that could produce saving faith, but also for the way in which

---

[46]*Christian Baptist,* February 2, 1829.

[47]Walker, *op. cit.,* p. 55. See also *Millennial Harbinger,* 1831, pp. 368-369; 1841, pp. 404-407.

this testimony was to be proclaimed, received, and acted upon. The most zealous of those who entered upon this quest was Walter Scott. As early as the third issue of the *Christian Baptist* (November 3, 1823) he was hot upon the trail. Under the pen name of "Philip" he wrote, "In spite of the discrepant and inapt schemes of sermonizing that now prevail by means of learned and popular establishments, there yet exists a certain, uniform, authorized plan of preaching Jesus, a plan consecrated by the high examples of all the heavens, and the holy apostles and prophets."[48]

Later he wrote, in the same series, " . . . there is but one authorized way of making Christ known to men, in order that they may believe and be saved."[49]

The centerpiece of this divinely authorized plan was the truth of the "Golden Oracle," that Jesus is the Christ, the Son of God. "The scriptures disclose this secret and lift it high above all the revelations of God. It is the very sun of the spiritual system. Shut your eyes to it, and Christianity is a most dark and perplexing scheme. Once behold it, and you behold the most certain and substantial argument for love to God and men."[50]

It is the Lordship of Christ, and that alone, that unites Christians. Moreover, "The Scriptures propose the belief of this fact . . . as the only means for increasing the body or church of God."[51] The gospel is a question of fact. "Is Jesus the Son of the living God or is he not?"[52] Belief, then, becomes a matter of fact, established by evidence, for "no one thinks of crediting a mere assertion."[53]

---

[48]"On Teaching Christianity—No. 2," *Christian Baptist*, November 3, 1823.

[49]*Christian Baptist*, February 2, 1824.

[50]*Christian Baptist*, November 5, 1824.

[51]*Christian Baptist*, November 3, 1823.

[52]*Christian Baptist*, January 5, 1824.

[53]*Christian Baptist*, February 2, 1824.

After the writing of his series "On Teaching Christianity" the exact steps in the divinely authorized plan eluded Scott for nearly four years. They evidently fell into place on September 16, 1827, during a private conversation with Jacob Osborne and Adamson Bentley following a meeting of the Mahoning Baptist Association at Braceville, Ohio. His first effort to preach it at Steubenville, Ohio, shortly thereafter failed, but on November 18, 1827, at New Lisbon, Ohio, he was successful. Thereafter, to the end of his life, he held to that date—November 18, 1827—as though it were the most important since Pentecost, for on that date, after being lost through all the dark ages, the ancient Gospel was restored!

Perhaps a brief review of that singular sermon is in order. Its text was from Matthew 16:16, "Thou art the Christ, the Son of the living God." The Golden Oracle! This was the fact which the four gospels were written to establish, he said. Type and prophecy had pointed to it down the ages. When Peter had proclaimed it, Christ had promised him the keys of the kingdom. When it became clear to the assembled multitude on Pentecost that Jesus was in truth the Christ, they cried out in great and earnest agony, "Men and brethren, what shall we do?"

Thus with flashing eye and impassioned manner, as one who would carry the whole present back into that inspired past, or make it live in a hushed present, Scott answered, "Repent, and be baptized every one of you in the name of Jesus Christ for the remission of sins, and ye shall receive the gift of the Holy Ghost."

"The conditions are unchanged! The Word of God means what it says!" Scott challenged. "To receive the word is to obey, and to obey is to do what three thousand anxious souls did in response to the invitation of Peter. . . . Is there any man present who will take God at his word and be baptized for the remission of sins?"

A candidate, William Amend, presented himself; Scott, startled at his own success, took his confession of faith in Jesus as the Christ and that same day baptized him in the local stream.

Later Scott wrote, "I proceeded in this matter without example, without counsel, and without reference to any mode or practice which I had ever heard of. I followed Christ and his Apostles alone, and the experiment was crowned with complete success."[54]

All Disciples of my generation are fully acquainted with the six steps of "the divinely authorized plan" as Scott outlined it. Reducing it to a convenient "five-finger exercise," Scott bequeathed it to a host of eager preachers who carried it to the four corners of the country and well into the twentieth century. In my own boyhood church I was brought up on it, as, I suspect, were many who hear this lecture. For the few who may not have done the five-finger exercise when they were young, let me repeat it beginning with the thumb, combining the last two of the six steps to fit the little finger: "Faith, repentance, baptism, remission of sins, gift of the Holy Spirit and life eternal."

Perhaps I can explain it no more briefly than in the words of the biography of Scott which I prepared in 1946:

> Now the pattern was revealed. After the evidence of Jesus' Messiahship was presented, first came *faith*, or believing the evidence; then followed in logical order, *repentance, baptism,* the *remission of sins, the gift of the Holy Spirit,* and *life eternal.* There were three things for man to do: believe, repent, be baptized. There were three things that God, through Christ, promised to do: remit sins,

---

[54]Scott's *Evangelist*, I (1832), p. 94. The New Lisbon incident is adapted from Stevenson, *Voice of the Golden Oracle* (St. Louis: Bethany Press, 1946), pp. 66-68.

bestow the Holy Spirit, grant eternal life. Here were all the elements of the ancient gospel, as preached by the apostles; and this was their proper order. Just as one needs all the right letters to make a word and then must arrange them in the proper order to spell that word correctly, even so one needs for the restoration of the gospel both the right elements and the right arrangement of those elements. Those doing these things in that sequence constitute the ancient order; they are the church![55]

Informed of Scott's evangelistic methods in a letter from J. E. Church dated July 28, 1829, Barton Stone found it to his own way of thinking and consistent with his practice. "I have no doubt but that it will become the universal practice though vehemently opposed."[56] Stone's numerous evangelists adopted Scott's "plan," and it became the general practice of both Disciples and Christians even before the merger of the two movements. And Campbell, not as literal as Scott, nor as enamored with an exact date for the restoration of a gospel lost for ages, approved the method. Writing an open letter to William Jones in the December issue of the *Millennial Harbinger,* 1834, he explained *"our manner* of preaching the *word."*

> Our evangelists . . . after proving that Jesus is the Messiah, and laying before the audience his person, office and character, and exhorting the persons addressed to put themselves under his guidance; tender an invitation to all present who have not yet put on Christ . . . After testifying and exhorting, if any persons come forward and thus acknowledge Jesus, confessing him to be both Lord and Christ, and avowing their intentions to become citizens of his kingdom, we, on confession of faith, immediately, or as soon as practicable (by night or day) take them to the water and immerse them . . . This is the *application* of our discourses. In this way we soon know, and the people know

---

[55]Stevenson, *op. cit.,* pp. 62-63.

[56]A. W. Fortune, *Adventuring with Disciple Pioneers* (St. Louis: Bethany Press, 1942), pp. 35-36.

who believe and repent, and who do not . . . Thousands
have been brought thus into the kingdom who now rejoice
with joy unspeakable and full of glory.[57]

6. *Forms of "preaching" and "teaching" derived from
biblical models.* We do not go very far with the fathers in
the pursuit of biblical models until we are forced to make
a distinction between "preaching" and "teaching." Modern usage identifies preaching with the sermon in the
Christian congregation. To get the perspective of Campbell and the others we have to set this modern view aside.
Studying the New Testament models, they came to the
conclusion that "preaching" was always directed to outsiders for the purpose of converting them; such "preaching" was never directed to insiders, who, as believing
Christians, were rather in need of "teaching."

Writing in 1862, Campbell expressed a view which he
had held for at least forty years: "There was *teaching,*
there was singing, there was praying, there was *exhortation* in the Christian church; but *preaching in the church,
or to the church, is not once named in the Christian
Scriptures!*" On the contrary, "We *preach* the gospel to
unbelievers, to aliens, but never to Christians, or those
who have received it."[58]

In what must be assumed to have been early Disciple
practice, Campbell in an earlier article (1853) delineated
some of the differences between "preaching" and "teaching": "The *preacher* singly aims at the conversion of his
hearers, while the *teacher* intends the development of a
passage, a doctrine, a theory; or in vindicating the tenets
he has espoused, . . . The preacher reclaims the heart;
the teacher cultivates the understanding and enlarges the
conceptions of his pupil. The preacher aims at producing

[57]*Millennial Harbinger,* 1834, pp. 589-590.
[58]*Millennial Harbinger,* 1862, p. 154.

faith in his auditory; the teacher at imparting *knowledge* to his disciple. . . ."[59]

This fine distinction was not observed by the sects: "The Methodist system has little teaching but much preaching, presuming that they often need to be converted." Since Congregationalists and Presbyterians are "for the most part in the church before they are regenerated . . . most of a pastor's labors are those of a missionary" to his own church.[60] By preaching to the unconverted on the biblical patterns, the fathers hoped to make Christians of them at the beginning of their church membership; and by teaching them after they were baptized they expected to edify them as a church body and strengthen them as practicing Christians.

The distinction between the functions of preaching and teaching occasioned a distinction between Christian ministers—one class of men to serve "at home" in the congregation, another class to serve "abroad" in the world.[61]

"Evangelists, as the term indicates, are persons devoted to the preaching of the word, to the making of converts, and the planting of churches."[62] They might be sent out by a single congregation or by several congregations acting in concert. In this connection it is helpful to remember a formula:

Evangelist = Preacher = Missionary

The teaching ministry beyond the early stages of a local church's establishment was performed by a plurality of local elders or bishops, elected and ordained by the

---

[59]*Millennial Harbinger,* 1853, p. 546.
[60]*Millennial Harbinger,* 1853, p. 548.
[61]*Christian System,* XXV:VI, p. 79.
[62]*Ibid.*

congregation. They had three duties: (1) to teach, (2) to rule—or "oversee," the literal meaning of "bishop," (3) to shepherd—or visit.[63] Thus, for the internal ministry of the church we get a matching formula:

Elders = Bishops = Pastors = Teachers

From this review, it may be supposed that we should get two main forms of Christian proclamation and instruction. Actually we get three. The third form was "exhortation." Unlike the others, this was addressed both to outsiders and to insiders. The warrant for exhorting outsiders was taken, like the model for so much else in the Disciple movement, from the Book of Acts, specifically from Peter's practice on Pentecost, Acts 2:40: "And he testified [i.e., preached] with many other words and exhorted them, saying, 'Save yourselves from this crooked generation.'" The warrant for exhorting *insiders* was found in passages like Titus 2:5. "Declare these things; exhort and reprove with all authority." 1 Thess. 5:14: "And we exhort you, brethren, admonish the idle, encourage the faint-hearted, help the weak . . . " Heb. 3:13: "But exhort one another everyday, as long as it is called 'today,' that none of you may be hardened by the deceitfulness of sin."

Having, then, not two but three forms of Christian oral address, let us say a few words about each of them:

Preaching. Stone, Scott, and Campbell held essentially the same views here. Preaching was to be done by itinerant evangelists, on models discovered in the Book of Acts, and, to a lesser degree, in the Letters of Paul. "Pagan eloquence" was renounced. In a series of seven articles, "The Christian Preacher" in 1832, Campbell studied the principal speeches of Acts, analyzing them in some detail.

---

[63]*Millennial Harbinger,* 1835, pp. 504-507.

He concluded, for example, that Peter's sermon on Pentecost, "was all logic, reason, point, testimony, proof. There was no declamation, noise, tinselling, painting, and mincing in the set phrase of the rhetoricians of the world."[64]

In No. 3 of this series, Campbell outlined the main features of a typically sound gospel sermon, as he derived it from these apostolic models. It would move through five stages:

First, the preacher states his proposition, for example, "Jesus is Messiah, the Son of God."

Second, he illustrates or expounds the principal term of the proposition. In the example, these are: "Jesus," "Messiah," and "Son of God."

Third, he proves the proposition. "The law, the prophets, John the Baptist, Jesus, the Apostles; the miracles, prophecies, labors and characters of the first heralds, furnish the arguments in chief which prove his proposition; and when documents are logically and scripturally presented, the proposition is proved."

Fourth, he will apply the proposition, in this case: ". . . sinners are persuaded to embrace him as Messiah, and submit to him as the Son of God."

Finally, he issues the invitation.[65]

Such preaching, however, was a part of a whole pattern of evangelistic activities which are compressively outlined in Campbell's seventh article, in which he described the work of an ideal preacher for whom he coins the name "Evangelicus." (1) Coming into a new community, Evangelicus first visits the Christian believers enlisting their support for the upcoming meetings; these are to pray for it and help publicize it. (2) In the meeting itself, running to three or four sessions, he "presents the testimony of the Messiah." (3) When this is done, he asks for

---

[64]*Millennial Harbinger*, 1832, p. 310.
[65]*Millennial Harbinger*, 1832, p. 231.

a division of the house. All who believe the testimony are asked to stand or to move to one side. (4) Evangelicus then concentrates upon those who made no response, asking them to state their reasons and objections to which he addresses himself. (5) Next he turns to the believers, asking them if they are willing to repent of their sins and "receive Jesus as Saviour of the world." Again he asks for objections which he tries to answer. (6) Speaking now to the reluctant and to the unbelievers, he begins to exhort. He addresses them "with all feeling, in the language of the warnings and denunciations of the Saviour and his Apostles . . . not to reject the counsel of God. . . ." (7) He then baptizes the converts. (8) Thereafter, on successive days, he teaches the converts the "constitution, laws, ordinances of the Christian kingdom." (9) Between meeting times he visits in the homes of the new converts imparting Christian instruction family by family. (10) After setting things in order, he moves on to the next town, (11) returning occasionally by the churches which he had planted. In this way Evangelicus plants churches at the rate of a dozen per year.[66]

It is interesting to notice that the preacher turns teacher in the initial phases of the new congregation's life. Not all evangelists did this well. Moreover, the lack of a settled, educated local ministry was a serious defect of the whole system. At any rate, Campbell warned against evangelizing without appropriate follow-up in teaching and organizing: "He is a worthless shepherd," he said, "who marks his lambs and turns them out into the forest to shift for themselves." "Some who call themselves evangelists," he cajoled, "more strikingly resemble the ostrich than the first preachers. The ostrich drops its egg in the sand, and leaves it to the sun and the sand . . . to take care of it; and

---

[66]*Millennial Harbinger*, 1832, pp. 469-471.

then itinerates the desert. . . . You galloping itinerants, see your prototype, and reform!"[67]

Exhorting. What was exhortation? The answer can be briefly stated in principle from the two pages in the *Millennial Harbinger* on "Order—as Respects Exhortation." There Campbell said, "A *preacher* proclaims *facts* and proves them by *witnesses*; a *teacher* ascertains and develops *truth,* and supports it by *arguments;* an *exhorter* selects *duties,* and recommends and enforces them by *motives.*"[68] Sometimes, but not often, gifts for preaching, teaching, and exhorting could be found in the same man. They were "not the same office, nor the same work." In any case, "The preacher and the teacher should always be followed by the exhorter; for all faith and knowledge are for corresponding practice."[69]

To see these principles in action we turn to Walter Scott. Joseph Gaston, one of Stone's Christian preachers, accompanied Scott for three weeks in 1827 just to do the exhorting at the time of the invitation following Scott's sermons. William Baxter wrote that Gaston "was highly gifted in exhortation, and his prayers seemed to be the natural outpourings of a warm and pious heart."[70]

Scott often used his young theological students as exhorters. Riding along to a meeting, he is reported to have said to one of these, "Now I will tell you how we must do; I will preach and you must follow in an exhortation; I will strike at the head, and you must strike at the heart, and *cry if you can.*"[71]

---

[67]*Millennial Harbinger,* 1835, p. 527. See also Barton Stone's *Christian Messenger,* Vol. 15, p. 11, and Walter Scott's *Evangelist,* Vol. 4, pp. 93-94.

[68]*Millennial Harbinger,* 1835, p. 487.

[69]*Millennial Harbinger,* 1835, p. 488.

[70]William Baxter, *Life of Elder Walter Scott* (Cincinnati: Bosworth, Chase and Hall, 1874), p. 149.

[71]Baxter, *op. cit.,* p. 257.

Best of all, perhaps, is an eyewitness account of Scott himself in the exhorter's role. He had called a meeting at Carthage with several distinguished Disciples as preachers—John T. Johnson, Benjamin Finnell, John O'Kane, L. H. Jameson, B. U. Watkins and several others. Scott presided. Johnson and O'Kane preached. Others led singing and exhorted. Meeting in the grove by day and in a schoolhouse at night, there were three services daily. "The woods were literally full of people." At the Sunday evening climax "invitations were given, songs were sung, and earnest exhortations were offered, but not a soul moved."

Then Scott arose. He had taken no part in the preaching or exhorting of this meeting, he said, because he had thought it possible that he himself, as the resident Carthage pastor, was an obstacle. "But now, after all that has been said and done, I have come to this conclusion, that your stupid indifference is not owing to any objections you have to me, nor yet to the men who have been laboring before you, but solely to your own cruel hard-heartedness." He sought then to shame and arouse them: "What can be the matter with you? Is it because you are destitute of common intelligence? Or is it because you are utterly careless of your eternal interests?" The entire exhortation, as remembered by L. H. Jameson, is reproduced by Baxter. Though brief, it is too long to quote in its entirety. Let one short passage suffice:

Are you disposed to defy the Omnipotent to arms? To engage in fearful and unequal war with the Eternal? To hurl yourselves against the bosses of Jehovah's buckles, and so to meet certain and eternal overthrow? He calls in mercy tonight; how can you dare to refuse? He stretches out his hand; how can you disregard him? Are you not afraid to trifle with his grace? Are you not afraid that he will break forth upon you like a lion, and rend you to pieces? Are you not afraid that he might come suddenly forth out of his place, and cut you assunder, and appoint you your portion with hypocrites and unbelievers?

Jameson's account of Scott on this occasion is instructive: "The manner of the speaker was all that the utterances required. Sometimes it was as gentle as the evening zephyr, in a moment a dark cloud, flaming with lightning, overshadow the heavens, and the rushing storm was heard, leveling everything in its course; then, gentle, and tender, and inviting again."

And the result? "The entire audience was astir. The first notes of the song were scarcely uttered before some of the best citizens of the place presented themselves to make the confession."[72]

Teaching. What was teaching? It was defined as "didactic discourse" to be conducted in the church as a school, two hours each Lord's Day. Having studied their lessons beforehand, members were to carry their Bibles to church and to "attend to all readings, teachings and exhortations . . . book in hand!"[73] The "president for the day" would deliver a lecture lasting about half an hour.[74] The order of this lecture, as outlined by Campbell, would be: (1) Exordium or introduction; (2) Proposition; (3) Illustration (if needed); (4) Proof; (5) Application—"press its moral or religious obligation upon the hearer, by the authority of its truth, and the magnitude of the motives which it suggests."[75] Following the lecture, the congregation joined in. In the "Extra" for 1833, Campbell gave a full-scale example of such group study, using Matthew 2 for demonstration purposes. He listed twenty-nine questions which Disciples, with the aid of "books and helps,"

---

[72]Baxter, *op. cit., pp.* 242-244. Account by L. H. Jameson.

[73]*Millennial Harbinger*, 1853, p. 551.

[74]*Millennial Harbinger, ibid.*

[75]*Millennial Harbinger*, 1835, p. 486. "Order as Respects Didactic Discourse."

were supposed to answer. Such a program pursued with persistence would create a church membership "fully literate in biblical knowledge":

> Intelligent in the Holy Scriptures, clothed with the armor of light, every disciple going forth will be a David against the Philistines . . . And, better still, the words of heavenly favor dwelling in his heart, he will carry with him in every society a fragrance like the rose of Sharon. . . .[76]

7. *Lay preaching*. One consequence to be expected from this whole approach was a tremendous increase in the amount of lay preaching. Local teaching within the congregations was largely in the hands of lay elders—ordained men, to be sure, but men who made their living at other vocations. Many laymen also took up the evangelistic trail. Among these was former lawyer and U. S. Congressman John T. Johnson. (Johnson, incidentally, was a member of the House of Representatives when Andrew Jackson received a plurality of the popular vote for the presidency but fell short of the necessary electoral votes in his contest with Henry Clay, John Quincy Adams, and William H. Crawford. Johnson voted for Jackson, who lost that time, as John Quincy Adams was elected.)[77] John Henry, a farmer, became celebrated on the Western Reserve as "the Bible with a tongue in it."[78] Amos Allerton was another farmer who gained like fame.[79] And there was Samuel Church of Pittsburgh. By the age of forty, he had read the New Testament one hundred and fifty times, the Old Testament seventy-five times.[80] The

---

[76]*Millennial Harbinger*, 1833, p. 373. For other articles on teaching, see *Millennial Harbinger*, 1835, pp. 486-488, 505, and *Millennial Harbinger*, 1853, pp. 541-554.

[77]John Rogers, *Biography of Elder J. T. Johnson* (Cincinnati: By author, 1861), p. 19.

[78]Baxter, *op. cit.*, pp. 143-147.

[79]*Ibid.*, pp. 172-175.

[80]Stevenson, *Voice of the Golden Oracle*, pp. 40, 173, 191.

68702

church at Deerfield, Ohio, sixty members strong, was said to have sixty preachers.[81] There were many strengths in this, but also some serious weaknesses. For example, by 1831 there was reported to be only one full-time preacher among Disciples in the whole Western Reserve.[82] Not only were local churches lacking in the ministry of settled pastors giving it their full time, evangelists were also struggling against severe financial limitations.

Walter Scott in the issue of his magazine, *The Evangelist*, for July 6, 1835, told of a Brother Taffee of Wilmington, Ohio, who had been State's Attorney for Clinton County. He gave up his law practice and went to preaching. He founded seven churches who were tardy in paying him anything. When they did pay him it was only $200.00, presumably his income for a year. In this same issue Scott addressed himself directly to evangelists:

> Beloved brethren, we are not quite ignorant of the numerous frauds which are played off upon you [in financial matters] in consequence of the infantile state of the churches and the introduction of imprudent and covetous men into them. Some of you have already been compelled to quit the field, and in doing so have gone to the study of law, or medicine, or returned to the mechanic arts, or to husbandry.[83]

Not only was there financial trouble for conscientious evangelists, there was also trouble for conscientious congregations in the persons of impostors and mountebanks who bilked them. On more than one occasion, Alexander Campbell found it necessary to warn the readers of the *Millennial Harbinger* against itinerant impostors. In Octo-

---

[81]Scott's *Evangelist*, Vol. 2, p. 52.
[82]Stevenson, *op. cit.*, p. 118.
[83]*Evangelist*, IV, p. 165.

ber, 1837, he published a letter of warning from Lewis County, Kentucky:

> A few weeks ago a young man of light complexion, light hair, somewhat inclined to curl, five feet and eight inches high, and calling himself *Henry C. Gilbert,* made his appearance in Lewis County, under the mask of a preacher of the Ancient Gospel. To some of the less informed brethren he produced a letter, which could not be read in consequence of the badness of the writing; but when more inquisitive and better informed brethren desired to see it, he at first pretended he had lost it, then positively declined showing it, and finally left them just before the time appointed by him for a two days' meeting; and has been heard of since making his way up the Ohio canal.[84]

In the December issue of the same magazine, Campbell published another warning, this one over his own initials:

> Brother Shepard of the "Primitive Christian," New York, has published *J. H. Lampear,* now in Portage County, Ohio, as a polygamist and unworthy of the name Christian. He is from all accounts, certainly unworthy the confidence of the Christian community as a *teacher* of religion. I trust I shall not be sued for this notice, as in the case of W. W. Sleigh. Impostors must be exposed and Christians protected from wolves in the garb of sheep, at all risks and perils.[85]

To clear up the reference to Campbell's being sued by W. W. Sleigh, I should say that several years before Campbell had accused W. W. Sleigh, a traveling religious lecturer, of swindling and embezzlement, whereupon Sleigh sued Campbell for $10,000 "damages to his fair name and reputation." The trial commenced in the Supreme Court of Pennsylvania, but was settled by arbitration requiring no less than thirty meetings over a period of about four years. It was not closed until August 4,

---

[84]*Millennial Harbinger,* 1837, p. 480.
[85]*Millennial Harbinger,* 1837, p. 574.

1838, when Campbell was successful in making his charges stick.[86]

These were growing pains of a new movement, in part; but they were also caused by a lack of tightening up at the point of the education and ordination of Disciple ministers. Preachers of Stone's Christians were sometimes as free-lance as Scott's, but Stone saw the need to put controls upon men who were "impressed with the belief that they are called to preach the gospel." If they were genuinely gifted men, "possessed of correct information or knowledge," and "endowed with a capacity of communicating that knowledge to the edification of their hearers, the church should encourage such to exercise their gifts in their meetings—*in their meetings;* for such speakers should first learn at home, in the church of which they are members, before they go abroad to preach; nor should they go abroad as preachers until they are sent and recommended by the church."[87]

The issue thus raised was not solved until the Disciples had passed through the power struggle of the postbellum period between lay elders and "the one-man system" of settled ministers. The resolution of the tension carries us beyond our present study.

For the rest, let it be said that the problem of impostors among the American Disciples was no worse than that of the false prophets in the early church, several times mentioned in the New Testament. And the problem of mutual ministry and lay preaching was certainly no more vexing than that encountered by Paul in the church at Corinth.

---

[86]*Millennial Harbinger,* 1836, pp. 91, 548; 1838, pp. 462-465, 478. Material credited in notes numbered 83, 84, and 85 are used by permission of Abingdon Press from my book, *The False Prophet* (Nashville: Abingdon Press, 1965), pp. 16-17.

[87]*Christian Messenger,* Vol. I (Feb. 24, 1827), p. 80, "Thoughts on Preaching."

Even with these problems, it was possible for the fathers to keep on believing that they were on the way to the church that was baptized with power on Pentecost. And they continued to follow their dream of the "amelioration of society" and the renovation of the world through the preaching of the Gospel Restored and the reestablishment of the Ancient Order. We are the heirs of that early, hopeful period so full of energy and pioneering zeal. It may sometimes have been naïve and visionary, but men in those days never entered a pulpit or stood on a wagon bed in a grove preaching to a crowd without expecting great things to happen.

APPENDIX:

A Modern Vindication
of Campbell's Theology
# of Preaching

Campbell's view that *preaching* was for the world, and not for the church, and that *teaching* was for the church, but not for the world, is not generally upheld by modern practice. And, in some quarters, it is even discounted in theory, the position being that preaching can occur only "in the congregation."[1] Campbell's position is supported, however, by such learned opinion as that of C. H. Dodd, the British New Testament scholar.[2] And it is vigorously upheld in a crusading pamphlet, *Christ's Preaching—And Ours*, by Michel Philibert, professor of philosophy at Grenoble.[3] Should the views of Dodd and Philibert—and those of Campbell—be taken seriously by the modern church, they would entail nothing less than a revolution in the practice of the average parish minister and congregation.

According to Philibert, Christ's *preaching* always moved toward the people in the world, finding them in their own situation. There it announced to them the good news of

---

[1] As in Jean-Jacques Von Allmen, *Preaching and Congregation* (London: Lutterworth Press, 1962).

[2] See Dodd's classic, *The Apostolic Preaching and Its Developments* (Edinburgh: R. & R. Clarke, 1936, and New York: Harper & Row, 1957).

[3] (London: Edinburgh House Press, 1963), translated by David Lewis from the French, *La Prédication de Jésus et Nous* (Paris: La Société Centrale e'Evangélisation de l'Eglise Reformée de France, 1962). Quotations by permission of Edinburgh House Press.

God, to which they were asked to react in personal decision. They were not given an indefinite period in which to
decide, but, since Jesus' preaching was *itinerating,* he was
always about to move on to other people. This moving on
to others was not merely for the sake of the others, but
just as urgently for the current audience, who were thus
forced to make their decision while they had the opportunity.

Those who decided for the gospel became disciples.
These Jesus *taught. Teaching,* however, was different from
preaching in that it took disciples and moved them from
their situation in the world toward their Teacher—toward his mind and spirit, and even in their occupations
and use of time. Teaching was further different from
preaching in that it was reiterated, being patiently re-
peated so that the disciples became schooled in their new
way of life.

> The aim of teaching is not to announce God's decision
> and to call for man's decision, as in the case of preaching.
> It is to make a new man of the disciple and enrol him in a
> team, this enrolment being itself, moreover, one of the
> means to his renewal. The disciple's emotional attitudes,
> behaviour, and understanding need reeducation. He must
> be given new standards. This is a slow process, calling for
> much patience, and effective only in small groups. It calls
> for intimacy, for the sharing of tasks and responsibilities,
> of risks and hopes, of joys and sorrows, for shared effort
> and shared relaxation, for common worship and prayer to-
> gether. A break with the old circle and its customs, with
> the character shaped and shut in by it, is demanded if the
> new man is to be born, grow and develop.[4]

Jesus' preaching was always accompanied and illumined
by his works of mercy and healing for the people to whom
he preached. And, as it developed, Jesus' preaching was

---

[4]*Ibid.,* p. 13.

nourished by the circumstances it encountered in the response of the people, which was not always that of joyous acceptance, but was often that of rejection and even of persecution. "Persecution accompanies preaching, as its shadow."[5] But, more than that, persecution provides the setting in which the claim of Christ is laid upon the conscience of the hearer so that he cannot escape it.

Teaching, which follows preaching as its natural consequence, is not merely for the sake of making disciples more and more Christian in themselves. It is also for the purpose of engaging them in Jesus' own mission—that of preaching and serving. The disciple begins very early in his instruction to share his newfound life with others; and that is a further means to his instruction. "Knowledge which we keep to ourselves remains sterile even for ourselves."[6] It is clear that the "preaching" of the disciples that Philibert is here describing is nothing as formal as "sermons" with "texts." It is done informally in all kinds of settings, often involving no more than two people, the disciple and his friend in the world with whom he is talking. It began with the hearer in his own situation and with what he knew and experienced and thus led him to the new and the unknown. When teaching is undertaken in the church, it is largely for the sake of arming the disciples for their mission in the world. Given that purpose, it takes on an urgency and has a vitality that it does not presently possess in the "religious educational" programs of the churches.

It is only when we have taken a candid look at Christ's preaching that we come to see ours in its true light as a crippling distortion of its original. By preaching, we do not ordinarily mean Christian proclamation informally

[5]*Ibid.*, p. 23.
[6]*Ibid.*, p. 29.

given in a worldly setting. Instead we "commonly mean
the sermon, the homily delivered in church during worship, and addressed to a Christian congregation."[7]

"Whatever other purpose the Sunday sermon may serve,
it usurps the function of preaching without fulfilling it,
and lacks the essential characteristics of preaching."[8] The
sermon, by being addressed to "habitués" and "sermon
tasters," loses its edge. The hearer makes no decision because he knows the preacher will be back at the same old
stand next week; so he can go on postponing his decision
indefinitely while appearing to be listening and even obey-
ing. "Indeed, the 'faithful' in general share in neither the
preparation, nor criticism, nor furtherance of the preaching. By a radical perversion, they have become merely the
recipients of preaching, and no longer those who relay
it."[9] Thus it comes about that "The Sunday sermon is
an illusory substitute for preaching." Not only so, it is accompanied by a corresponding deterioration in teaching.
The minister does not even think of himself as a teacher;
and the attender does not take himself seriously as a disciple. "Instead of 'living' in Christ, they [churchgoers]
vegetate,   atrophy,   and   become   sterile,   unfruitful
branches." Such teaching as the minister does under these
circumstances is apt to be "abstract and remote, designed
to enrich leisure moments, but demanding no real sacri-
fice of time or habit on the part of its recipients."[10]

Deterioration in preaching and teaching is, not surpris-
ingly, accompanied by a deterioration in service. The
church turns "narcissisticly in upon itself." It preaches
the gospel to itself, and not to the world and in the world;
likewise, its works of mercy are often "confined to giving

---

[7] *Ibid.*, p. 38.
[8] *Ibid.*, p. 38.
[9] *Ibid.*, p. 39.
[10] *Ibid.*, p. 41.

assistance to its own members."[11] The result is stagnation. Adults cease to grow. The church settles down into routine ways. Imagination withers. Invention dies. "Instead of multiplying, and recognizing the signs of the Kingdom of him who makes all things new, instead of remaining responsive and inventive, alert to the fresh needs and new aspirations of men, instead of letting themselves be renewed by the conversation which they ought to keep going between the world and God, the churches and their charitable organizations are too often preoccupied with self-preservation."[12]

With all of this Alexander Campbell would have been in hearty agreement. If it sounds radical and if it portends a revolution in church life, once it is taken seriously, it is an index all the clearer of our errant straying from the path of the fathers. Their way courted the dangers of lay excesses and frontier disorder, but it was bursting with life. Our way invites the opposite and more fatal dangers of formalism, clericalism, bureaucracy, and ritualistic sterility. It may not be amiss for us to go back to our beginnings for a time, that we may go forward more surely.

[11]*Ibid.*, p. 43.
[12]*Ibid.*, p. 44.